A Holistic Approach for Cultural Change

A Holistic Approach for Cultural Change

Character Education for Ages 13–15

Marc Levitt

ROWMAN & LITTLEFIELD
Lanham • Boulder • New York • London

Published by Rowman & Littlefield
A wholly owned subsidary of The Rowman & Littlefield Publishing Group, Inc.
4501 Forbes Boulevard, Suite 200, Lanham, Maryland 20706
www.rowman.com

Unit A, Whitacre Mews, 26-34 Stannary Street, London SE11 4AB

British Library Cataloguing in Publication Information Available

Library of Congress Cataloging-in-Publication Data

Names: Levitt, Marc Joel, author.
Title: A holistic approach for cultural change : character education for ages 13-15 / Marc Joel Levitt.
Description: Lanham : Rowman & Littlefield, [2017]
Identifiers: LCCN 2017005858 (print) | LCCN 2017021350 (ebook) | ISBN 9781475835960 (elec-
    tronic) | ISBN 9781475835939 (cloth : alk. paper) | ISBN 9781475835946 (pbk. : alk. paper)
Subjects: LCSH: Moral education (Secondary)—United States. | Social change—United States.
Classification:LCC LC311 (ebook) | LCC LC311 .L48 2017 (print) | DDC 370.11/4—dc23
LC record available at https://lccn.loc.gov/2017005858

♾ ™ The paper used in this publication meets the minimum requirements of American
National Standard for Information Sciences Permanence of Paper for Printed Library
Materials, ANSI/NISO Z39.48-1992.

Printed in the United States of America

To Nicole Piscionere,
who has demonstrated how to be a great middle school librarian

Contents

Preface

In 1988 at the Democratic National Convention, then Texas agricultural commissioner Jim Hightower said that George H. W. Bush was a person "born on third base who thought he had hit a triple." While lampooning the president's privileged background and his ignorance about how his family's money and connections made his rise in politics possible, Hightower also inadvertently pointed out a blind spot in the American psyche, the mistaken belief that we live outside of our social and/or environmental context. This idea, that we are, as Paul Simon famously said, "rocks" and "islands," rather than rhizomes, birthed from and giving birth to, other roots and rhizomes, obfuscates how we are social creatures, needing each other for everything from intimacy to vocational success.

We are moved by the caring acts of others and empathize with their emotional struggles. We smile at a chance encounter with a "consequential stranger" and we are grateful for those whose lives touched ours in meaningful and inspiring ways. And yet, in spite of this, we hold tightly to our belief that we are autonomous creatures, living essentially without being affected by and not affecting others.

Consequently, in school, when we "teach" character education, it is too often through the use of admonition, as if we are trying to "tame the beast" in ourselves, rather than by building on our pro-social proclivities and our innate understanding that indeed, "we are all in it together."

In *A Holistic Approach for Cultural Change: Character Education for Ages 13–15*, we will look at how our curriculum and its delivery supports the interpretation that we are inherently isolated and competitive individuals. Through stories, tips for classroom conversation, and curriculum and pedagogical suggestions, I will try to help educators help their students to recognize and act with the understanding that we are interdependent and that actions are not without consequences, both to others and to oneself.

At the age of twenty-three, after a childhood filled with idolizing heroic cowboys, soldiers, and baseball players and a teenage and early twenties filled with romance for great artists and revolutionary leaders, I believed I was destined to be yet another solitary hero. I wasn't very happy and felt isolated and trapped within my own thoughts, dreams, and aspirations.

One spring, 1973 day, in San Francisco, I left my work as a teacher in a "feminist/socialist parent co-op" and walked into a park and sat. I was locked inside a spinning fun house of thoughts, trapped in my own isolation. I was living inside a room of reflecting mirrors, captive of an unending loop of thoughts and questions. I asked myself the essential question, "Who am I?" and realized that my goals for my life were restricted by my romance for the autonomous heroes of my youth. I realized that if I continued to live in this way, I would live bereft of real human contact.

My goals were almost immediately transformed from those generated by what I call "Shallow Individualism," the belief that we are self-contained individuals operating in a world of other autonomous humans, to ones birthed by "Deep Individualism," the recognition that the true fulfillment of an individual life lies in the understanding that we are truly "all in it together." Personal fulfillment was no longer generated by a childhood dream of heroic isolation but upon recognizing and acting upon my permeability, vulnerability, and the need for others.

After a lifetime of working at the intersection of arts, humanities, and education, here is how I have come to look at how we, as educators, can help our students prepare for a world where interdependency is not only a philosophical concept, but an issue of individual well-being and indeed, planetary survival.

Introduction

It is difficult to judge how much of a problem bullying actually is. So much of it goes undetected in both manifestation and ramification, perpetrated behind corners, in secluded environments, through the Internet. So much gets unreported because of fear, its accepted "normality," and/or from the hope that it will eventually end.

Are bullying, teasing, and so forth more present now than ever, or are we just speaking about them more? Do new technologies and distribution systems like Facebook and Twitter make bullying more pervasive or are we exaggerating its extent? Are kids becoming less sensitive to others as their worlds become more confined to their homes and screens? Is the proliferation of adult-driven activities as opposed to "free" play in the neighborhood, rendering the skill of negotiating differences and compromise, vestigial, no longer needed when adults are making the rules? Is our nation's increasing income disparity and the anxiety it fosters leading to more stress within households, contributing to more violence outside?

These questions are probably unanswerable. Certainly, though, it is irrefutable that teasing and bystander behavior is occurring. Whether bullying is increasing or not and why is another book, one that requires a different competency than that of this author. Instead, this book is more interested in helping you to help your students understand that their well-being and the well-being of others are linked together and that acting from this understanding will benefit them at school, at home, and in their community. Additionally, this book is interested in helping educators be aware of how they are inadvertently helping to create the very behavior they want to eradicate, through what is being taught and how.

Student behavior as well as your school's curriculum is nested within a larger societal cultural narrative. Children internalize the behavior and behavioral expectations they see in adults and notice within the media. Young people make choices about who they are and how they are expected to behave through a complex dance that includes the instinctual, psychological, and social, all of whose borders are actually quite porous.

Curriculum is created, chosen, and distributed in ways that reflect everything from how its writers perceive the world, to the politics and economics of textbook adoption. Complex and at times contradictory narratives are built into what we "digest" through advertising, mass media, means of control at home, work, and play, as well as the content of a school's curriculum and the way it is distributed. These messages, subtle and not so subtle, affect everything from who we are and how we behave, to how we interpret what being "human" is all about.

In an August 2016 study by John Ifcher of Santa Clara University and Homa Zarghamee of Barnard College, "The Rapid Evolution of Homo Economics: Brief Exposure to Neoclassical Assumptions Increases Self-Interested Behavior," they found that "even brief exposure to commonplace neoclassical economics assumptions moves behavior toward self-interest."

In other words, the authors found that learning that self-interest—or better said, "shallow self-interest"—is "rational," led students to act "selfishly". It left little room for contemplating behavior embedded in an alternative understanding of our motives and proclivities, ones that foreground the common good and an awareness of our interdependency.

In spite of our well-intentioned interest in creating a positive school environment, one where harmony, peace, and diversity celebration are priorities, these goals are often contradicted and ultimately thwarted by the way these goals are shared and the content and distribution of the rest of the school curriculum. To be even partially successful in creating an atmosphere where student behavior is changed from "me first" to "your health is my health" we must align our pro-social messages with the content and distribution of the rest of the curriculum. As Marshall McLuhan said, "The medium is the message."

Our society's dominant cultural narrative, the story that frames how we think about who we are, what stories we tell about ourselves, and what motivates much of our behavior toward one another is a narrative that derives in large part from what I call "Shallow Individualism." This philosophy is based on our understanding that we are separate and discrete entities making our way in a world of other separate and discrete entities, in which "nature" is distinct from "self" and where we are in constant fear of shortage, calamity, and Hobbesian-type chaos.

This belief posits a competitive model to survive, one where there are winners and losers. Obviously this is not the complete story about how we perceive the world nor does it accurately depict how we behave. We care for our families, friends, neighbors, and coworkers and understand their importance in our lives. We are exalted by nature's beauty and understand how air and water pollution can affect our heath and happiness. Nonetheless, for the most part, in the United States, our national anthem, the song we march to, is essentially the "late period" Sinatra anthem, "My Way."

Individualism's emphasis on acting according to our own internal mandates is not without its important historical role. The freedom to set out on one's own, outside superstitious, unnecessarily restrictive, and often capricious boundaries, enforced by "inevitability," and/or physical and psychological power, based on class, caste, race, family, gender, sexual choice, and so on, was truly liberating.

In our contemporary society, however, Individualism has morphed into a perversion of a genuinely liberating philosophy. While Individualism had and probably still has an important role to play in freeing us from unnecessary and/or unwarranted restrictions, as well as serving as the basis for much of the Universal Principals of Human Rights, it has created a world in its most extreme image.

We have become blind to what we have in common, to how much we need one another, and to the effects our actions have on others and ultimately on ourselves. We have become blind to how all of our fates are linked. The power of "Shallow Individualism" has also obscured our innate understanding of how we learn socially, need each other for our happiness, and are in continuing dialogue with "nature."

"Shallow Individualism" is at the foundation of our curriculum and pedagogy. When we study history, we too often learn the stories of socially decontextualized "great" men (usually men and White men at that). We view nature as something outside of ourselves rather than with the understanding that we *are* nature, in continual dialogue with all else on this planet and probably beyond. We don't teach subjects from a systems or an ecological point of view, but instead teach as if one subject is separate from another. Our testing models are predicated on sorting and pitting one against the other, rather than on supporting cooperation and the success of all.

The results of teaching from this perspective is at variance with what we say we want to accomplish with our social curriculum; getting along, working together, and valuing differences. It's a contradiction to teach cooperation in a school where there are few opportunities to work cooperatively. It is very difficult to celebrate diversity when very few types of intelligences are venerated, utilized, or assessed; when the stories of so many are invisible. It is practically impossible to understand that actions have consequences when we teach subjects as impenetrable fortresses impervious to their "surroundings."

Our school culture, its pedagogy, and its curriculum not only reinforce our inherent competitiveness and our illusion of our own isolation, but also don't take advantage of our students' visceral understanding of empathy and their enjoyment of cooperation. Consequently, when teaching character education, we have no recourse but admonition and threats.

If we are to avoid an admonition-based, top-down approach in our attempts to create a sustainable culture of caring in our schools, we need to find ways to build upon our students' "better angels"; to reinforce our students' visceral understanding that the culture they create is the one they inhabit. This type of school finds ways to appreciate and utilize the talents of all, to render visible cause and effect and the permeability of illusory "borders" and teaches intellectually and viscerally, how we are, as a species, equally, if not more so, predisposed to cooperation than we are to competition.

The good news is that in science and human relationship theory, it is becoming more and more acknowledged that our happiness and well-being *is* dependent upon each other's happiness and well-being and that it is as "natural" to cooperate as it is to compete, both in human and animal worlds. We are connected biologically and psychologically and just as we are hardwired for competition, we are also hardwired for cooperation, compassion, forgiveness, altruism, generosity, and empathy and in fact our survival has long depended upon it. Here is some literature that supports this point of view:

- In two anthologies, *Prosocial Motives, Emotions and Behavior: The Better Angels of our Nature*, edited by Mario Mikulincer and Phillip R. Shaver (American Psychological Association, 2010) and *The Compassionate Instinct: The Science of Human Goodness* , edited by Dacher Keltner, Jeremy Adam Smith, and Jason Marsh (W. W. Norton & Company, 2010), the authors write about research into these and other areas of what is often referred to as "Pro-Social Behavior," behavior that derives from our innate and perhaps even genetically encoded understanding of how important it is for our species' survival to simply get along and cooperate.
- In Rebecca Solnit's superb book, *A Paradise Built in Hell: The Extraordinary Communities That Arise in Disaster* (Viking Adult, 2009) she looks at how after our twentieth-century natural and human-made disasters, individuals spontaneously formed "communities of help" without government aid. Ironically, soon after they did, "forces of order" like the military, whose homes were far from affected communities, with little or no contact with local residences and who operated from a Hobbesian paradigm, interpreted these communities of help as possible sites for anarchy. Expecting the worst of people in crisis, they shut down many of these helping communities and imposed a "top-down" model of aid.
- Matt Ridley's *The Origins of Virtue* (Penguin Books; Paperback 1st edition 1998) argues that cooperation and self-interest are not in conflict.
- In *A Cooperative Species* (Princeton University Press; Reprint edition, 2013), Samuel Bowles and Herbert Gintis discuss how society builds institutions around altruism and cooperation to perpetuate itself.

- Christopher Boehm, director of the Jane Goodall Research Center and professor of anthropology, in *Moral Origins: The Evolution of Virtue, Altruism, and Shame* (Basic Books, 2012) looks at how our morality has evolved as a necessity and often through peer disapproval with antisocial behavior as a survival technique.
- Paul Seabright in *The Company of Strangers: A Natural History of Economic Life* (Princeton University Press, 2010) looks at how trust and interconnectivity are evident in the species even within finance and our vast networks that produce and distribute our needs.
- Elinor Ostrom, the first woman to receive a Nobel Prize in economics, studied how individuals in different parts of the world work together to prevent the destruction of what they have in common.
- Frans de Waal is a primatologist and ethologist. *Peacemaking Among Primates* (Harvard University Press; Reprint edition 1990) perhaps locates the biological roots to conflict and reconciliation and looks at the peacekeeping techniques of primates.
- Yochai Benkler's book *The Wealth of Networks* (Yale University Press, 2007) looks at how informational technology supports and itself is based upon collaboration. He cites *Wikipedia*, Creative Commons, Open Source Software, and the blogosphere as examples.
- David Bollier, an American activist, writer, and policy strategist, has written a number of books on the "commons," that is to say, what we share, utilize, and collectively take care of for our mutual advantage.

When Nicholas A. Christakis, a physician and sociologist and professor at Harvard University, and James Fowler, an internationally recognized political scientist who is an associate professor of political science at the University of California, San Diego, announced their finding of a study they made about the roots of happiness with a group of 4,739 people followed from 1983 to 2003, as part of the famous Framingham Heart Study, it sent waves through the mainstream media.

Our happiness is determined by a complex set of voluntary and involuntary factors, ranging from our genes to our health to our wealth. Alas, one determinant of our own happiness that has not received the attention it deserves is the happiness of others. Yet we know that emotions can spread over short periods of time from person to person, in a process known as "emotional contagion." If someone smiles at you, it is instinctive to smile back. If your partner or roommate is depressed, it is common for you to become depressed.

But might emotions spread more widely than this in social networks—from person to person to person, and beyond? Might an individual's location within a social network influence their future happiness? And might social network processes—by a diverse set of mechanisms—influence happiness not just fleetingly, but also over longer periods of time?

[The people they studied were] embedded in a larger network of 12,067 people; they had an average of 11 connections to others in the social network (including to friends, family, co-workers, and neighbors); and their happiness was assessed every few years using a standard measure.

We found that social networks have clusters of happy and unhappy people within them that reach out to three degrees of separation. A person's happiness is related to the happiness of their friends, their friends' friends, and their friends' friends' friends—that is, to people well beyond their social horizon. We found that happy people tend to be located in the center of their social networks and to be located in large clusters of other happy people. And we found that each additional happy friend increases a person's probability of being happy by about 9%. For comparison, having an extra $5,000 in income (in 1984 dollars) increased the probability of being happy by about 2%.

Happiness, in short, is not merely a function of personal experience, but also is a property of groups. Emotions are a collective phenomenon. (www.edge.org/3rd_culture/christakis_fowler08/christakis_fowler08_index.html)

These books and this study are rooted in an understanding that we are connected to one another and that our well-being depends upon the well-being of others. If we as educators base our teaching styles, our pedagogy, and our content on this understanding, we can change our school environment and dare I say it, our global culture, to one where happiness, success, safety, and the fulfillment of being human can be derived not from competition, not from a fear-based model, but from one that supports our inherent connection to all that we are linked to.

We will probably never be able to completely eliminate bullying, teasing, snubbing, passive bystander behavior, and so on, but we can help our students understand that it is not the only strategy available to survive and indeed to flourish.

A short story: Five poor brothers who lived and always ate dinner together could only afford four rolls each day from the market. Each dinner was a source of anxiety. Each brother plotted ways to get one of the four rolls and not be the one who was left with none. It was not unlike a game of musical chairs. Dinner was *never* pleasant! One day a stranger passed through the village, knocked on their door, and asked if he might spend the night and have some dinner. The brothers looked at each other and their immediate thought was, "Now, instead of one being left without a roll, two would be!"

They got progressively more and more nervous just thinking about this. As they sat at the table, the brothers were twitching with anxiety as if they were at the starting line of a race. Each brother was anxiously waiting to grab a roll. Suddenly, the stranger reached out both hands and took the rolls, putting all four of them on his plate. The brothers sat silently, aghast at this stranger's audacity. Suddenly the stranger took his knife and cut each of the four rolls into half and then two of those halves, he cut in half. He gave a half a roll to each brother and to himself. Then to each, he gave the smaller portion, so each of those around the table got three quarters of a roll.

The brothers looked at each other and smiled at how lucky they were to get not only one piece of a roll but two! From that time on, each of the brothers got something and none were left without! Everyone agreed that after that, dinners were a lot more fun!

Please, let's not get caught up in whether or not this "enlightened" solution to the above problem could ever really be achieved in "real life." The point of this story is to demonstrate the differences in approaches between Shallow and Deep Individualism, between a solution based on short-term gain and one based on an understanding of "Mutuality of Interest." Whether or not it is possible to ever get your class, grade, school, community, nation, and/or world to behave according to the latter is impossible to predict. To make space for its possibility is what is important.

This book is about helping you think about, plan, and distribute a curriculum that makes visible how one person's well-being is ultimately another's. *A Holistic Approach for Cultural Change: Character Education for Ages 13–15* suggests curriculum and pedagogical changes that will help your students recognize that bullying, teasing, isolating, passive bystander behavior, and expressing and acting upon fears about all kinds of diversity is not just "bad" but ultimately not in anyone's best interest. This book is about helping you create a curriculum and a method for its dissemination that will help your students remember that we are all social beings who need each other to learn, play, survive, and create to reach our fullest potential.

A Holistic Approach for Cultural Change: Character Education for Ages 13–15 is not a book filled with admonition, but rather, a book that attempts to make an understanding of "Mutuality of Interest," the guiding principal in the behavior of students. It is a book of theory and of practice; giving a philosophical foundation to its point of view, while making very practical suggestions. Its goal is to help students make behavioral choices where individual goals and the needs of others no longer seem contradictory.

Culture change is not simple and can't be accomplished only through posters, speeches, and/or an occasional speaker. It needs to be embedded into the everyday interactions between student and student, teacher and student, staff and student, between your administration and faculty, into your curriculum, and woven into your pedagogical approach.

HOW CAN YOU USE THIS BOOK?

In *A Holistic Approach for Cultural Change: Character Education for Ages 13–15* , there are personal narratives as well as original, folkloric-type stories about a variety of topics pertinent to character and social issues. There are

stories about bullying, teasing, gossiping, rumors, snubbing, bystander behavior, boy-girl relationships, forgiveness, vengeance, diversity, empathy,
cooperation, stubbornness, embarrassment, and sharing. After each story
there are questions for students to think, write, and talk about pertaining to
the issues addressed. There are also suggestions about how to integrate the
lessons of these stories into your curriculum and its delivery system. You can
pick stories at random, or read the stories in the order that I have given them.

May you enjoy using this book and that after you do, may admonitions
like, "Do unto others as you would have them do unto you" and "Ye reap
what ye sow" become no longer Sunday school platitudes, but as real as a
cement truck. Karma is physical and tangible, whether or not you believe that
the results of one's action will come in this life or another.

Good luck.

Chapter One

The Bridge under the Highway Overpass

Connecting Neighborhoods and People

When Alan was thirteen, he belonged to a gang. It wasn't a very tough gang, though. They walked together down the street asking each other questions they imagined would be their exams. But of course, they liked to think of themselves as "tough." Their imagined toughness came from numbers. The "Lucky 13," as they called themselves, would go everywhere together . . . all together, all thirteen of them. They'd take the subway to the Ranger, Knick, Met, and Yankee games. They'd go bowling and get pizza every Friday after school. They'd go to the movies every Saturday and play ball on Sundays.

But, in this crazy, not as tough as they thought world of the "Lucky 13," they'd prove their toughness by what they loved doing the best (Drum roll, please!)—being thrown out of places. Yes, you read this correctly. They had fun getting themselves kicked out from any place they could get into or at least look into. It didn't matter from where: movie theaters, bowling alleys, pizza parlors.

On Saturdays they'd go to the movies. In those days the films were either Westerns, World War II films, horror films, or Jerry Lewis comedies and there were usually two films for one price—a double feature! Before the film there would be a black-and-white newsreel that was like network TV news today, but much, much more dramatic. A man's deep voice urgently or humorously told viewers why the event they were watching was important. Sometimes, there were even cartoons before the main feature as well.

A "matron," who was an elderly woman with a flashlight, would show them to their seats in the "children's section" and as soon as the flashlight went out and left, "fun" would begin . . . talking, laughter, making fun of pompous politicians and celebrities on the screen, tossing candy or popcorn, and soon the complaints from people who wanted their moviegoing experience undisturbed by thirteen-year-old boys. The woman who guided them into their seats would be summoned and they would quickly be removed from the theater.

Sometimes they pretended they wanted to stay, only because they liked arguing and then, a young man, whom they last saw taking tickets, would come down the aisle with a bored look on his face and yet with a bit more authority than the "matron," and insist that they leave. From there, a wave of energy would take them to a pizza place, a laundromat, a clothing store, a diner and they'd look at a person eating and pretend to cry or they'd laugh. It wouldn't take long before someone would come out from the kitchen, from the back of the store, and invite, or rather order them angrily to leave, sometimes gently and sometimes with a push that would almost knock them to the ground. This was the first part of their Saturdays.

Now, every "gang" needs a gang to be its enemy. They had one and they were located in Corona right next to the community of Forest Hills where the "Lucky 13" lived. Corona was under the highway from Forest Hills, a highway that took people from Manhattan to points east, to Long Island, and back. In Forest Hills, the kids were primarily Jewish, Italian, and Irish. In Corona, they were Puerto Rican. The kids from Forest Hills barely knew where Puerto Rico was (the Caribbean Sea), nor did many of them know that it was an island (it is). They just knew in Puerto Rico they made kids "different" from them. How? They were, as the "Lucky 13" imagined, more vicious and mean than people from the fifty states.

They had heard rumors that the last kid who made the mistake of going under the highway overpass from Forest Hills to Corona was kidnapped, beaten into something resembling hamburger meat, rolled into a ball, and attached to a flagpole and left there as a warning to future "invaders." They had heard that a group of kids from Corona had one time charged under the overpass into Forest Hills and into a local school's kindergarten class, taking five kids from there and never returning them!

They hated the Corona guys and were sure that the feeling was mutual. On Saturday after being kicked out of enough places, the "Lucky 13" would go down to that overpass and almost like clockwork, the "Corona Gang" (that's what the "Lucky 13" called them) would be there waiting. The roar from the highway traffic was loud and a large puddle of water was always under that overpass, one that soaked the feet of the tired senior citizens who lived in Forest Hills and shopped in Corona.

The "Lucky 13" glared at the "Corona Gang" who glared back and both gangs just stood there until someone said, "Come on over, if you are so tough." "Oh yea?" "You come over first" . . . And then more staring until

Alan, the leader of the "Lucky 13," moved toward the puddle as if he were going to cross into Corona until he was inevitably pulled back by one of his "boys." Then, another kid from the other side of the "puddle," who appeared to be the leader of the "Corona Gang," would aggressively come toward the "Lucky 13," only to be pulled back by his "boys."

And so it went each Saturday. . . . Kicked out of the shops and theaters, the threatening looks and posturing inevitably ending when they all got bored, or when they had to go home for dinner. They hated each other, almost like the Jets and the Sharks did in *West Side Story*, except without the knives, the girlfriends, or even a real fight. But it didn't matter to them . . . it all felt very real.

As spring emerged, Little League baseball began. Alan had played for years with kids from all over the borough of Queens, New York. He loved playing and in some way it didn't really matter whether he won or lost. He just loved to play and he liked that he had a completely different group of guys to hang with other than the "Lucky 13." One of those guys was a kid named Chico Ruiz. He played shortstop and was probably the best ballplayer in the league year after year. He was quick, with sure hands and a rifle for an arm. Alan and Chico played together on a lot of different teams over the years and when Alan showed up for his first practice, there was Chico. They were going to be teammates.

"Hey, Alan," Chico said. "Good to see you! Next week I turn thirteen. Here's directions to my house. I'm having a party and I'd like you to come."

"Sure," Alan said, not really wanting to commit to coming to the party.

Chico sensed that. "You've gotta come!"

"OK, I promise," Alan reluctantly said.

That afternoon, after baseball practice, Guttstein ran into a couple of the "Lucky 13s" who were getting pizza. They spoke for a while and then Alan pulled out the directions that Chico had given to him earlier.

"Yea, I got to go to a party here next week."

They looked at it, sat silently, and one of them, "Johnny B," as he was called, said, "You can't go to that party."

"Why not?" Alan asked.

"Because that party is in Corona!"

"But I promised," Alan answered.

"I know, but you know what happened to the last kid from Forest Hills who went over to Corona. . . . Chopped up like hamburger meat and attached to a flagpole!"

"I know, but I made a promise."

"OK then, we'll all go with you."

Alan understood at that moment that one of the great things about being in a "gang" was to have people to watch your back and make sure you were going to be all right, whatever stupid thing you did.

So, the following Saturday, after getting thrown out of two theaters (a new one, down the street from the Midway had just opened), one Italian restaurant, a florist, and a jewelry store, the "Lucky 13" walked to the highway overpass. There, as usual, was an elderly woman trying in vain not to get her shoes wet as she made it through the puddle to get into Corona. Alan walked under the overpass, into and through the puddle, and into Corona. He was finally "there," entering what for all of his "boys" was a foreign country and their worst nightmare. Corona on the mind, threateningly filled with "wild" inhabitants, roaming lions, rogue elephants, and rushing hippos waiting to pounce on his innocence.

Alan turned to thank his friends for making this journey with him, but as he did, he realized he was all alone. None of his "boys" had made the trip across the "border" and there he was, for the first time, standing alone in a land that had existed only in his fears—Corona!

Johnny B yelled, "Hey, if you need us, just yell. We'll be there."

Alan walked slowly at first, not sure whether he should continue or return to the safety of his home community. He followed the map Chico had drawn on the invitation. Left, right another right . . .

Have you ever gone into a new neighborhood and you knew from the houses, maybe the streetlights, the people, that you were somewhere different and because of that difference, it was much scarier than the comfort and familiarity of your own neighborhood? This is how he felt in Corona, where the two-story, two-family houses were different from the six-floor brick apartments where he lived in Forest Hills and where the language of the writings in the store windows were not in the Italian and Hebrew of Forest Hills, but in Spanish, and where colorful streamers decorated storefronts and old men played checkers and dominoes, dressed in tank tops as they sat on stools in front of houses.

Alan made a left, another left, a right, and realized that the neighborhood had changed again, from residential to what looked like small factories with their clanging noise of metal hitting metal, with steam climbing up through small tin chimneys and with the smell of paint fumes and automotive oil everywhere. He realized soon, too, that he was lost! It didn't seem to matter which direction he turned. None looked promising, so he walked to the right and in front of him was a guy in a T-shirt, bent over, pulling a tire off its rims. Alan asked him for directions but the man shook his head in a way that clearly said, "No English."

Alan kept walking and realized that there were others on this road, coming toward him. There were five boys, one of whom was dragging a baseball bat on the ground. Alan turned to the left, walked a half a block, and there were three more boys walking quickly toward him. He turned completely around and there were four boys, one of whom carried a baseball bat, walking toward him and then another turn and again, two more boys walking toward him.

Luckily he noticed a road cutting off at a diagonal and he began to run down it, believing it would be his escape, but at its end was a twenty-foot-high concrete wall! Alan turned back toward where he had come and by now, the four tributaries of anger, the four groups of boys had merged and they had become a raging river of violence walking determinedly toward him!

He knew he had no choice. He sat on the cement street, covered his head, and realized that he was about to be the next kid from Forest Hills to make the mistake of getting lost in Corona and that after the beating he was going to receive, he would be on that flagpole to serve notice to others from across the highway overpass never to make that journey into Corona.

From down on the ground, Alan heard the sound of the sneakers squeaking on the cement street as the boys headed toward him. He heard the sound of the bats scraping against the asphalt, the sounds of Spanish, and as the boys hovered above him, he felt the hot breath of their anger.

He sat there, waiting to get his beating, when he heard one of the boys say, "Are you Alan?"

He slowly removed his hands from his head.

"Yes."

"Chico sent us to look for you. He thought that you might get lost." Alan looked up. Those boys were looking down at him with a mix of curiosity and humor. A couple of them who were standing above him, he recognized as members of the "Corona Gang." The one who'd said his name offered his hand to get Alan off the ground and they began walking.

Moving street to street, the neighborhood appeared different from how he'd imagined it and how he experienced it at first. The small, two-family houses that looked so unfamiliar were less strange. Boys and girls fixed bicycles, grandmothers dug into garden dirt, fathers and sons played catch, older kids polished cars, older boys and girls walked hand in hand. They arrived at Chico's house.

Chico came out to greet Alan.

"They found you?"

Alan just smiled.

"Hey, welcome. This is my mother, father, Pete, my brother, my sister, Angelina, my *Tia* . . ."

"Don't overwhelm him," said Chico's father, and Alan felt thankful for this.

"OK . . . you ever play soccer?"

"Nah," Alan answered.

"OK, let's go."

Alan played soccer and ate spicy food that day for the first time. Alan danced salsa and helped smash a piñata for the first time that day. The party was different from any he had attended in Forest Hills. There were many more relatives and the kids were not completely separated from the grown-ups. Chico's cousins were dancing with grandparents, his brother and mother were dancing, and his uncles and aunts, mother and father were all moving over the dance floor. Neighbors came by with food and presents.

Alan felt, as he was having one more piece of fried chicken, one more fried plantain, one more cup of lemonade, that he was really, really lucky . . . lucky to have been invited, lucky to be part of something he would never had been part of had it not been for Chico, lucky to learn that the world didn't begin and end with Forest Hills, and he understood, as well, that he was forever changed.

Just as his taste buds were now forever changed by the hot sauce he now generously poured on his beans, just as his feet after salsa dancing would never move the same way again, just as his kick of a ball would never again be toe first, just as he would never consider grown-ups always boring, he realized that he would never be the same either. From this time on, Alan understood that life's differences would never again be obstacles, but he would be able to embrace it as something he wanted, something that needed to be part of his life and to learn from . . . and then, a soccer ball hit him gently in the back of the head.

"Hey," said Chico, "Mom said I should bring you back to the overpass before it gets dark."

After saying goodbye to what seemed like a thousand people, Chico and some other kids walked him back to the highway. When there, a solitary elderly woman, her hands filled with grocery bags filled with food, made her way across the puddle. They looked at her for a second and Chico said,

"We should build a bridge over that puddle so the old people don't have to get their feet wet when they cross. Hey, you bring your group of guys over here next Saturday and I'll bring ours. We'll get some wood and tools and we'll build the bridge."

"OK . . . see you then . . . and thanks!"

"Glad you could come. See you then."

Alan waved goodbye and with a bit of sun left in the sky he walked through Forest Hills, toward his building. There were fewer people on the street in Forest Hills and it was quieter. He really missed the party's excite-ment. In his apartment, his mother and father were quietly reading and his brother was building a model airplane. The next day in school, the "Lucky 13" met on the schoolyard during lunch recess. He told them about the party. Some were interested, others didn't believe him, and still others wouldn't let his experiences break through their ideas about those kids from Corona.

"That hot sauce must have gotten to your brain."

Then Alan broke the real news to them.

"Next week, we are going to help them build a bridge over that puddle under the overpass."

"No way! I'm not going to help those kids build anything! My father said that they will steal everything from your pocket if they get you," said Pete.

"My dad said that it's the same now as it was when he was a kid. PRs are bad news!" said Max.

"Hey, I know and we know what those kids are like and I'm not going to work with them and catch whatever Spanish disease they have!" said Sean.

Alan realized that he could have said some of these things himself . . . before.

"Hey it's not like that. Don't worry."

The following Saturday they met at the Midway and were soon thrown out. They were kicked out of a few stores, too, before heading toward the highway overpass. About six or so of the "Lucky 13" left the group. Either they made up other things they had to do or their parents actually told them that they couldn't do anything with kids from Corona. Whatever. The rest walked down to the overpass. Some of Alan's friends seemed actually nervous.

By the time they arrived at the overpass, Chico and his friends had begun constructing the bridge with wood and tools they brought. They stopped, stood up, and for a second it seemed for a brief moment that time stood still and they all just stared at each other. Chico came toward Alan and they shook hands. He introduced his buddies and Alan introduced the "Lucky 7." He explained the work that they had done and the work that still needed to be done.

Without any direction, Alan's friends went over to groups of Chico's friends and pitched in with what needed to be finished. After three hours and after the final nail was hammered, after the final board attached, after the final piece of paper cleaned, what was now about seventeen coworkers stood back and admired their creation.

Just then, a couple, maybe eighty years old, approached the overpass from the Forest Hills side on their way to shop in Corona. They looked at the boys and they looked at the bridge and they looked at the puddle and did the same thing a couple of more times, until Chico said, "It's OK. You can use the bridge."

The elderly couple looked at one another and a moment later became the first ones to use that bridge, hanging tightly on to its railings. When they got across, they looked at the boys and waved and the members of the two groups applauded, slapped each other on the backs, opened up cans of soda Chico had brought. With that the bridge over the puddle under the highway overpass, connecting Corona and Forest Hills, was inaugurated.

After that day many people used that bridge. But it also turned out that the elderly weren't the only ones to use it. Chico and his friends from Corona used that bridge to come to Forest Hills to play basketball with the kids from Forest Hills on courts that were much better than those in Corona and the kids from Forest Hills used that bridge to cross into Corona to play football with the "Corona Gang," on a field that was much better than their own.

Recently, Alan went back to Forest Hills for the first time in many years. He went by that overpass wanting to see if the bridge his friends built was still there. As the traffic roared from above and as the old people walked from their homes in Forest Hills to shop in Corona, he saw that the bridge was no longer there. As he stared at where it once had been, he recalled the time it was built and he remembered how changed all of them were because of it.

He noticed the old people getting wet walking through that same puddle on their way to or from home or shopping, and although he was unhappy that their feet got wet without the bridge, it also felt good to realize that for him and hopefully for the "Lucky 13" and the "Corona Gang" that bridge would always be there, inside of their minds and hearts.

QUESTIONS FOR STUDENTS

- Have you ever had negative thoughts about certain nationalities and/or "races" and found that once you got to know people from those backgrounds you realized that your ideas about them were not accurate? If so, when?
- Have you ever heard friends and/or relatives speak badly of certain "kinds" of people? If so, what did they say?
- Did you ever say anything to those people who were talking bad about another group? Should you have and if so, what would you have liked to have said?
- What do you think is the best action to take when you hear someone insulting a person from another national or "racial" group?
- Where do you think the thoughts "The Lucky 13" had about Puerto Ricans came from?
- What helped Alan break down his prejudice?
- Have you ever been teased or excluded because of your background? What happened?
- Has anyone you know been teased or excluded because of the color of their skin, nationality, or religion? Tell us about it.
- Do you have family stories about relatives who have been teased, harassed, or discriminated against because of their national origins or the color of their skin? When and what happened?
- Have you ever made fun of someone's name, national background, and/or skin color and if so, why? How did it feel when you did?

THOUGHTS FOR STUDENTS

Many of us live in a place where there is very little diversity. We don't get to see, meet, and/or to interact with different kinds of people. We get our ideas and misconception of "others" through recycled stories via conversation and media that are often racially, ethnically, and religiously tinged by past misconceptions and fears, and which are sometimes created by those who were interested in separating people. These are not good ingredients for creating a society that understands how important it is to have diversity in your population.

What is prejudice? It is the "pre-judging" of an individual based on negative ideas about what that person is like, based on their skin color, national origin, and/or religion. We take these "stereotypes" and use them to make quick and easy judgments about what that person is "like"; whether or not we should be scared of them, whether or not you and your friends should see them as enemies, and whether or not we want to share our neighborhoods with them.

To stereotype an individual is to make a complex person, a person who has many parts, one-dimensional and to paint them with a broad brush by saying to yourself and others, "This type of person must be like this because he/she is . . ." You know what I mean. You probably have done that and you probably have heard others do that, even your older relatives, I'd bet.

These prejudices, these stereotypes are not only not useful, they are also dangerous and limiting for you and for our nation. Often prejudice toward certain groups have helped justify behavior that one would consider unthinkable. Colonialists justified taking the land of Native people by telling themselves that Native people were not sophisticated enough to maximize the land's potential. Americans justified enslaving others by saying that Africans were childlike and should be "taken care of." Europeans' stereotypes of Jewish people allowed many to blame the "Jewish bankers" for the Depression and used that scapegoating to eventually justify extermination.

That old chant "Sticks and stones will break my bones, but names will never harm me" is not really true. Not only will words hurt, but they also allow others to behave in ways and to create policies that will harm those who are being stereotyped.

As you saw in this story the prejudices of the "Lucky 13s" toward those who were or whose families were from Puerto Rico not only greatly limited their contact with them, but also fueled what could have escalated into violent confrontations. The lack of contact with the "Lucky 13" intensified the prejudice, permitting it to solidify the stereotypes. Once Alan finally went into Corona and visited Chico's house and met his family and friends, he realized how much "bigger" he became, learning from and enjoying his time with people whom he had previously considered a threat. Once he met them, the people from Corona were no longer just "ideas" generated from prejudice, but were "real" people.

How sad it would have been were Alan never to have that opportunity. How sad it is for all of us who limit ourselves because of our prejudices. Many think we should tolerate diversity. How about instead of tolerating it, celebrate it? It makes us smarter, culturally richer, and safer.

Why safer? This is one of the most interesting and overlooked parts of why diversity is good for us. When there is only one "type" of person around, be it color, nationality, gay or straight, girl or boy, interested in sports or arts, and so on, those with a different background, interest, gender, are more "at risk." They will be more easily identified as "different." In a diverse society, one where many different kinds people mingle, play, see, and watch each other, it is more difficult to single out one group for persecution.

As science progresses and as more and more work is done with DNA, it is becoming more and more acknowledged that there is no such thing as a "pure" culture. When we make fun of each other about our backgrounds, we are often teasing ourselves, since we all have a little bit of "everything" running through the basic building blocks of who we are. There is no such thing as a "pure" nation or a "pure" people. We are all mixes of various peoples from various lands.

What we think is pure "French" or "Spanish" is the result of putting comparatively new borders put around a geographical place that contained many different tribes of people, who perhaps lived in the region only for a while, who had family members from other geographic regions, and/or who probably never considered that they had something in common with others who became categorized as "this" or "that" nationality.

We are all "mutts" and the sooner we realize that, the more we can shake off our prejudices and get on with the joy of discovering who we are and begin to learn from one another. We need each other. We need our differences for our stories and wisdom, for our knowledge of living on the planet, and for our survival.

When the tsunami hit Thailand in 2004, there was a one tribe of people on a remote island whose population was saved. Those people had a folktale that warned its people to head up to the high ground when the water goes out too far. An elder who still held this story saw the water moving out into the sea. Remembering the story his elders had told him, he warned his people to move up the mountain and they did, saving their lives.

How many other stories, how much music, math, and science, ways to farm, to fish, to get rid of wastes, to build ecologically, plants to heal, ways to dance are there that we never will learn if we hold on to our silly prejudices and perpetuate the mistakes of the past. It is up to your generation to truly teach the world about how prejudice hurts and limits us all.

THOUGHTS FOR TEACHERS

Curriculum and Pedagogical Suggestions: American and Global History, Science, and Media Literacy

Recently the *New York Times*, *National Geographic*, and elsewhere reported on a study in *Science* magazine that through research done on the DNA of the Neanderthal that "modern" humans—or Homo sapiens—interbred with their Neanderthal neighbors, who mysteriously died out about 30,000 years ago.

"We can now say that, in all probability, there was gene flow from Neanderthals to modern humans," lead study author Ed Green of the University of California, Santa Cruz, said in a prepared statement. Damian Labuda of the University of Montreal's Department of Pediatrics and the CHU Sainte-Justine Research Center determined some of the human X chromosome originates from Neanderthals, but only in people of non-African heritage.

The article in Discovery news speculated that "the modern human/Neanderthal combo likely benefited our species, enabling it to survive in harsh, cold regions that Neanderthals previously had adapted to."

"Variability is very important for long-term survival of a species," Labuda concluded. Every addition to the genome can be enriching (http:// www.nytimes.com/2010/05/07/science/07neanderthal.html, http://news .nationalgeographic.com/news/2010/05/100506-science-neanderthals -humans-mated-interbred-dna-gene/, http://news.discovery.com/human/ge-netics-neanderthal-110718.html).

The online February 8, 2010, edition of the British paper the *Telegraph* reported that

> Archeologists have discovered the 2,000-year-old skeleton of an Asian man in an ancient cemetery in Italy, suggesting that the Roman Empire's reach was far more extensive than previously thought. Although the Romans are known to have traded for silk and exotic spices with China, it was thought that most of the commerce was conducted through intermediaries along the Silk Route and that no Chinese or other Asians entered the empire itself. (http://www. telegraph.co.uk/news/worldnews/europe/italy/7190020/Asian-skeleton-found-in-ruins-suggests-Roman-Empire-larger-than-thought.html)

The February 3, 2010, online Discovery news reported that

> DNA analysis of 2,000-year-old bones found in eastern Mongolia reveal a man of Western heritage.
>
> "Consider an older gentleman whose skeleton lay in one of more than 200 tombs recently excavated at a 2,000-year-old cemetery in eastern Mongolia, near China's northern border. DNA extracted from this man's bones pegs him as a descendant of Europeans or western Asians. Yet he still assumed a prominent position in ancient Mongolia's Xiongnu Empire," said geneticist Kyung-

Yong Kim of Chung-Ang University in Seoul, South Korea, and his col-
leagues.   (http://news.discovery.com/history/mongolian-tomb-western-
skeleton.html)

- Here are some of the "tribes" that have been consolidated into what we
  now consider "German": Franks, Saxons, Vandals, Lombards, Goths, Ala-
  manni, Franks, Chatti, Frisii, Sicambri, Thuringii, Huns, Celtics, Jewish,
  and Romans
- According to Ptolemy's *Geographia* there were around twenty different
  tribes in the area we now call England during its days of Roman occupation in the second century
- What we consider Spain is a soup of many "tribes" including Iberians,
  Celts, Romanized Muslim and Jewish cultures, Moorish, which has been
  called not a "distinct tribe," nonetheless seems to include Black Africans,
  Berber, and Arabic populations

It seems that most of the people on our planet are the result of the continual
mixing of various genetic ingredients that are still evolving. At the same time
there has been throughout history temporary solidifications of this fluid process, for political and/or economic reasons. At these times the illusion of
"purity" emerges and expresses itself as distinct "nationalities," cultural and
religious groups, and "races." At times the flowing river is mistaken for a
stagnant pond; the movie for a photo.

Our temporary national/religious/cultural affiliations and the power those
categories have on our imagination has led to misunderstandings, prejudice,
fear, exploitation, war, and genocide. At the same time these self-identified
borders can shift easily and quickly. An artist from Slovakia, Ilona Nemeth,
documented her grandfather's home of eighty years and showed how, during
this time, his home was, during various periods, part of three different countries or empires.

In another example of how fluid loyalties are, some nineteenth-century
German-Jewish immigrants to the United States maintained such a strong
sense of "being German" that, as the United States was thinking of joining in
the war against Germany in World War I, Americans often thought their
sympathies tilted toward Germany. Of course, another twenty years later,
there was no doubt where their children's allegiance lay.

Our belief that the temporary is forever, that "racial," cultural, national
identities are "fixed," that borders have been there forever, and that who we
are is a "noun" and not a "verb" is in my opinion one of the most tragic and
harmful delusions we have. This belief too often locks us into a cage. The
location of the key unfortunately appears unknown to us while in fact, it lies
within our own pockets.

The story above is just one very small example of how stereotyping is potentially dangerous and ultimately self-limiting. The lives of the kids from Forest Hills became richer once the backgrounds of those from Corona were not interpreted as negative but as positive. How much more interesting and richer their lives became when cultural heritage was no longer interpreted as a barrier to friendship, but as just another quality to share with one another, and how much richer their lives became when they could identify a common problem and work together to ameliorate it.

How can you help your students celebrate rather than be fearful of diversity? How can you help your students embrace rather than reject "difference"? How will students be able to realize that the world's diversity is a strength, rather than a symptom of a problem?

Teaching biodiversity as part of your science curriculum is one way.

A healthy ecosystem protects water resources, soil formation, nutrient storage, pollution breakdown, climate stability, food, medicine, and gene diversity. This understanding of mutual dependency in nature is a good introduction to how human diversity is important for our health and well-being.

In your history curriculum, teach students that what is now considered "fixed" is never really so. Studying history and geography is to study change. For instance, the idea of a "nation" is relatively new and the understanding that nations are permanent entities, filled with predictable and unified populations, is an illusion.

There is no such thing as race. The idea that certain categories of people, be it cultural, religious, ethnic, racial, all act in certain ways is simply untrue. We all share behavioral characteristics. Falsely attributing negative characteristics to a certain group because of the false belief that one group or another has a monopoly on what is deemed a "dangerous" characteristic has led to many of the horrors that our planet has seen. These incidences of "ethnic cleansing" or genocide should be studied by your students.

Of late, luckily, there has been a lot more attention and a lot less fear about admitting how diverse we all are. Societal admonitions against "mixed" marriages is not nearly what it once was. Lots more people consider themselves "multiracial." There has even been a great deal of pressure to make our US census categories more flexible, although they are not yet as flexible as they should be.

Studying the history of the census is a good place to start. It helps us understand how the categories that were created to sort and count are not "fixed" entities but the result of politics and cultural assumptions all rooted in particular times and places. It is also very useful to study the history of and admonitions against "mixed" marriages. After all, it was not until 1967 when the state of Virginia's law against "mixed" marriages was overturned.

In the United States and Britain at the end of the nineteenth and into the twentieth century a pseudoscientific theory about who should and who shouldn't breed flourished. This theory, eugenics, was widely accepted by academics and politicians in the United States and Europe and formed much of the theoretical basis for Nazism. It is a good idea to study the history of eugenics to help your students understand how a supposedly scientific theory based on falsely attributing characteristics to one group of people can lead to the horror of genocide.

There have been nations and cultures in the world's history known for their appreciation of the value of diversity, where intellectual traditions cross-pollinated and advances in the sciences, arts, and culture were made. While one has to be careful to not romanticize such places and periods, it nonetheless is true that Spain in the eleventh to the fourteenth centuries, the Ottoman Empire of the nineteenth century, Timbuktu in the fifteenth century, and New York City in the twentieth and twenty-first centuries were and are places and times where diversity was not only tolerated, but also facilitated and celebrated and where lots of mutual learning flourished.

Literature gives educators many opportunities to help students understand the experience of diversity, individually and culturally. There are many novels and memoirs that articulate the experience of being "mixed" and/or of trying to "pass" from one culture to another. There is also, of course, quite a lot of literature by individuals whose lives were affected by prejudice. This literature not only helps us understand how prejudice was and is experienced as an individual, but also how prejudice is internalized and can shape an individual's sense of who they are and how they participate in the society.

Look at languages for clues of our diversity. All languages are the result of the merging of many tribal languages. Yiddish, for instance, is a language born of the cross mingling of cultures: German, Polish, and Hebrew. Here's what *Wikipedia* has to say about it: "The historical language of the Ashkenazi Jews. It originated during the 9th century in Central Europe, providing the nascent Ashkenazi community with an extensive Germanic-based vernacular fused with elements taken from Hebrew and Aramaic, as well as from Slavic languages and traces of Romance languages." Yiddish words like "bagel," "chutzpah," and "schlep" are very much a part our English as are, of course, Spanish and Italian, to name a couple of influences.

But you can go back even further to find that the English language is even more of a composite than we think. Again, from *Wikipedia*, "Old English developed from a set of North Sea Germanic dialects originally spoken along the coasts of Frisia, Lower Saxony, Jutland, and Southern Sweden by Germanic tribes known as the Angles, Saxons, and Jutes. In the fifth century, the Anglo-Saxons settled Britain and the Romans withdrew from Britain. By the seventh century, the Germanic language of the Anglo-Saxons became dominant in Britain, replacing the languages of Roman Britain (43–409 CE): Common Brittonic, a Celtic language, and Latin, brought to Britain by the Roman occupation" . . . English "has changed considerably in response to contact with other languages, particularly Old Norse and Norman French, some scholars have argued that English can be considered a mixed language or a creole—a theory called the Middle English creole hypothesis."

And finally, if you have time, walk through your neighborhood and find ways your neighborhood is itself an example of many "tribal" influences. These influences are everywhere, in restaurants, in the music you hear on the street, and in the clothes you see in the shops. Our world is a wonderfully colorful and diverse place and what's even better is that it is constantly being rewritten.

Chapter Two

Palisades Park and the Roller Coaster Ride of Having Pride in One's Heritage

Across from Queens and the East River (not really a river, but what they call a tidal straight) is Manhattan, and across from Manhattan and across the Hudson River is New Jersey. From Manhattan, New Jersey looked like the beginning of the America Burt saw in picture books and not the New York City he knew from his life in Queens. This America, the one that began with New Jersey, was an America of large mountains and small buildings. This America started with the Palisades, cliffs that rose from the Hudson River and looked like the walls of a medieval fortress, seemingly protecting the rest of the nation from the "evils" of New York City.

High on those cliffs was an amusement park, appropriately called Palisades Amusement Park. Palisades Amusement Park was the best amusement park in the New York City region. Sure, there was the legendary Coney Island and the short-lived Freedomland, but Palisades was better and even was celebrated in a song written by a guy named Chuck Barris, who later hosted a TV game show called *The Gong Show*. A guy named Freddie Cannon sang this very popular song.

> Last night I took a walk after dark
> A swingin' place called Palisades Park
> To have some fun and see what I could see
> That's where the girls are
> I took a ride on a shoot-the-chute
> That girl I sat beside was awful cute
> And after while she was holdin' hands with me
> My heart was flyin' up like a rocket ship
> Down like a roller coaster
> Back like a loop-the-loop

> And around like a merry-go-round
> We ate and ate at a hot dog stand
> We danced around to a rockin' band
> And when I could, I gave that girl a hug
> In the tunnel of love
> You'll never know how great a kiss can feel
> When you stop at the top of a Ferris wheel
> When I fell in love down at Palisades Park

Palisades Amusement Park, even advertised in Superman and Wonder Woman comics, was also known for its rock-and-roll concerts and for its catchy advertising jingle:

> Palisades has the rides . . .
> Palisades has the fun . . .
> Come On Over.
> Shows and dancing are free . . .
> so's the parking, so gee . . .
> Come On Over.
> Palisades from coast to coast, where a dime buys the most.
> Palisades Amusement Park.
> Swings all day and after dark.
> (bumm, baa, dumm, bumm, bummmm)
> Ride the coaster . . .
> Get cool . . .
> In the waves in the pool.
> You'll have fun . . . so . . .
> Come On Over.
> (dumm de dum da dum . . . dum)

Palisades Amusement Park was just far enough from Burt's home to be considered foreign and just near enough to be accessible. Burt had gone with his family quite a few times, but this particular Easter break it was the destination of choice for him and his friends. Easter break always fell at a funny time, a kind of "in between time." Even though it happens at different times of the year the weather every Easter vacation was always unpredictable. Sometimes it could be cold and drizzly, as if winter were angry about having to exit, and sometimes, the sun and flowers were already out and Burt and his friends were already playing baseball.

On this particular day, it was the former, cold and drizzly, the kind of day that if he didn't leave quickly, he would be stuck at home, watching TV reruns and playing with his younger brother. Burt was determined not to let that happen but he had to think of what to do. It was one of those days when baseball was out of the question, when football would be equally uncomfortable, and when all the kids had seen the movies at the local theaters. Burt ate his breakfast cereal with the radio on and then it came to him as over the radio he heard:

Palisades has the rides . . .
Palisades has the fun . . .
Come On Over.

Shows and dancing are free . . .
so's the parking, so gee . . .
Come On Over.
Palisades from coast to coast, where a dime buys the most.
Palisades Amusement Park.
Swings all day and after dark.
(bumm, baa, dumm, bumm, bummmm)
Ride the coaster . . .
Get cool . . .
In the waves in the pool.
You'll have fun . . . so . . .
Come On Over.
(dumm de dum da dum . . . dum)

He and his friends would go to Palisades Amusement Park!

Burt called around and by 8AM reached all of his friends—about ten of them. Some said right away there was no way their parents would let them go over to New Jersey with "just" a bunch of kids. Some said they would call back when they asked their parents and some said yes right away.

Burt packed his lunch. Usually, he wouldn't have bothered and would have had a hot dog at the park. But today was also part of the eight-day holiday of Passover, when Jewish people, like him, were supposed to eat a certain kind of flat and very, very dry bread called matzah. Jewish people ate it to remember when they were slaves, and they left Egypt in a hurry for freedom and didn't have time for the bread to rise. Burt put a couple of slices of bologna in between the matzos, put it in a paper bag with some cookies, and was off.

By nine, he was at the candy store above the subway station where they always met and by 9:20, Elston, Everett, Jeffrey, Bobby, Allan, and Charlie all had arrived. Everyone but Everett had lunch bags like Burt had. Everett was the only one who wasn't Jewish. They bought a newspaper and went down into the darkness of the subway station, bought subway tokens, and soon were on the platform, into the train and their Easter break expedition had begun.

This would be a complicated trip, but they had no worries, Charlie was a mass transit guru. His nickname was "E Train." He knew how to get everywhere within New York City and beyond. The kids even had a game when they were bored. It was called, "How d'ya get to?"

"E Train, how d'ya get from Yankee Stadium to the Polo Grounds?" Or, "how d'ya get from Forest Hills to Radio City Music Hall?"

Each time he was right . . . oh, there was one exception, when they decided to go from Yankee Stadium to the Staten Island Ferry and ended up in Coney Island. But other than that, they were always "home free" when they were with "E Train."

The boys stood in a train that was, while almost done with its rush hour work, still crowded, so they had to stand. They didn't mind. They liked holding on to the smooth bars, rocking back and forth, bumping purposefully into each other, like big puppies.

"OK," E Train said. "Next stop, 42nd, bus station."

Having by now completely woken up after the long train ride, the boys were exited to get out and to begin their adventure. No one quite knew how he did it, but "E Train" somehow found a way to navigate through one of the most complicated, ugly bowels of transit oblivion in New York City, passing rushing crowds of people, the stink of exhaust, and dozing passengers on hard plastic benches waiting for their buses. About twenty minutes after they arrived at the station, "E Train" had them at a gate that said "Palisades Park."

"It'll be here at 10:15."

And it was!

They boarded the bus, as did the crowd of mostly moms with kids with a vacation day to kill. They were really the only "independent" group of kids, other than a group of five girls who looked about fifteen, who began applying lipstick and eye makeup as soon as they got into the bus. The driver, a gray-haired man with a look of authority, started the bus and it roared and moved slowly forward, curved around a maze of roadway and soon, they were in the Lincoln Tunnel that went under the Hudson River and into "America."

Once out of the tunnel, it was clear that the weather wasn't . . . clear. The drizzle formed droplets on the bus windows and windshield. The windshield wipers went back and forth, back and forth, with the predictable slow moving pattern of a metronome keeping time to a waltz. The bus made its way on New Jersey roads, now wet and at times filled with puddles. It was not one the most beautiful rides they'd ever had. It kind of like one of those rides on a rainy day with your parents when all you can do is stare out the window wishing you were home in front of the TV. The girls in the back though were giggling as if it were a sunny day in the summer.

Burt and his friends stared out the window noticing the small rivulets of rainwater drip down the glass. It probably occurred to all of them that it might not be real fun to be at an amusement park on an early April day and whoops . . . who had suggested it? However, their mood changed, as did moods of all the little kids with their mothers, as they saw the first glimpses of the Ferris wheel and then the roller coaster. Suddenly the idea of an amusement park changed into a *real* amusement park. The bus choked and gasped its way into the parking lot and the guys gathered their lunch bags and headed out into the lot and into the park. By now there was just a slight mist in the air and it had warmed up, just a little.

The park, usually filled with their families on sunny weekends, was now pretty empty. There were other "roaming bands of kids," teenage boys and girls walking together into the line for the "Tunnel of Love" or to get on the Ferris wheel. All the rides seemed to be working as they walked around the park scoping out which ones to go on. Even in the drizzle, an amusement park shoots energy into one's bloodstream and their pace picked up as they went on and off the rides: the Cyclone roller coaster, the Wild Mouse and its breathtaking curves, the Round About whose speed created a very uncomfortable centrifugal force that pushed them back into uncomfortable metal "cabinets" as they were whisked around in a circle, the Airborne and the Twister. . . . Everett wondered whose job it was to come up with all these names and he decided it was the job he wanted when he got older.

As soon as they got off one ride, they went on another and as soon as they got off that one, it was onto a third. It might have been misty and drizzling. It might have been chillier than it was in the summer. They might be getting wet, but on this early spring day in 1962, one of the park's first days open dates of the year, those boys were having a great time.

They even saw those fifteen-year-old girls again. The girls had found, or the other way around, a group of six tough-looking black-jacketed sixteen- or seventeen-year-old boys. These guys all had the pompadour haircuts, popular back then with the "tough" or "hoody" crowd, and their pants were very tight! They smoked cigarettes as they flirted with the girls. They noticed the boys and went about going from ride to ride.

It was afternoon by the time Burt and his buddies realized they were hungry. Maybe it was seeing the waffles that they couldn't eat because of Passover. Maybe it was going past the dining hall and smelling the hot dogs and French fries, also not good for Passover. Maybe it was the cotton candy . . . good for Passover or not? But somehow, it didn't seem right for lunch.

The drizzle slowed to a mist and the boys found some benches to open up their bag of Passover-OK food. They removed their matzos, now cracked, and only small chips now protected their fingers from the bologna, which flopped like dead fish as they ate. As they sat, eating their lunches (Everett had gotten a hamburger, which the others eyed with envy), they noticed those teenage guys who had been flirting with the girls from the bus.

One of them seemed to notice that Burt was looking at them and he tapped his friends on their shoulders and pretty soon the rest of them were looking at Burt and the others. Burt tried to divert his eyes and pretend that they weren't still staring and was temporarily successful until the tough-looking teens hovered above Burt and his friends. They continued to eat.

"Hey," said the one that caught Burt's eyes. He had the beginnings of a little mustache. "Hey," he said again. "Are you ignoring us?"

Burt looked up.

"No."

"Then why aren't you looking at us," he said. The others, all equally as big, looked at each other and laughed.

"We were eating."

"Jew bread, huh?"

"I don't know," Burt said. "My mother packed it."

"You guys are Jews, aren't you?

"No, we aren't Jews," Burt said, as the tension between the older and younger boys thickened like cookie batter.

"How come you are eating the Jew bread, if you aren't Jews?"

"I told you. Our mothers packed it for us. Maybe it was the only bread in the store."

Just then another, bigger and far uglier boy said, "You're Jews and we don't like Jews here at Palisades Park."

Just then, E Train, who in addition to being a mass transit expert was the ultimate "wise guy," said, "That's funny because I heard that your mother married a rabbi."

That stunned the older kids for a moment, giving the younger boys just enough time for Burt to say, "Run!"

And they did . . . dropping their lunches and running as quick as they could to the parking lot and then to the bus that was luckily there waiting. They charged into the bus with those big kids still running behind. One of those boys, who had taken one of their fallen matzos sandwiches, threw it at the bus and as Burt got into his seat he watched it slide down the wet window to the sides of the bus and then to the wet ground. The bus started up and in silence they rode back to the bus station. During the ride back to the candy store where the day began again, none of them said a word. Burt walked alone to his home.

When he got home, the house was cleaned, "company coming" cleaned, and he remembered that people were coming over for Passover Seder, the dinner at which you eat special foods, sing special songs, and remember to be thankful that the Jewish people came out of slavery. He also understood it as a celebration of the Jewish people and taking pride in their ancestry.

Slowly, his uncle, grandparents, and then friends of his mom and dad arrived and they began, as the sun set, to read the Haggadah, the book about the story and rituals of the holiday. They drank grape juice and ate the Passover food. Burt felt funny to be there in his apartment, dressed up, just a few hours since being at Palisades Amusement Park. They read the Haggadah, about the history of Jewish slavery and about the creation of the Jewish people after forty years of roaming the desert. In spite of being bored and hungry, Burt thought about those forty years wandering around in the desert, with the heat or the sun and without food, except the miracle food, manna, that God supposedly provided. Burt thought for a second that these people, way back, without a home, except for the tents they stayed in every night, they were his ancestors.

As he imagined their lives and then the lives of his father's parents who had come from Russia, escaping persecution and who took in laundry to iron and clean, and his mother's family who came as immigrants from Germany and England and the religion that kept them all together through more difficult times than he probably would ever have to experience, he couldn't help but be embarrassed about what he said that same day at Palisades Amusement Park, when he denied who he was and those who came before him.

QUESTIONS FOR STUDENTS

- Have you ever been afraid or embarrassed to admit some part of who you were? When did it happen and do you know why?
- When Burt said that he wasn't Jewish, did you think that was a smart or a stupid thing to do? Why or why not?
- Would you have done the same? Why or why not?
- How can we handle it if someone is threatening us because of something we are and can't and/or don't want to change?
- Have you ever threatened someone because of their background or for something they couldn't change? When, how, and why?
- Have you ever heard adults use bad language about certain groups of people? How did that make you feel?
- What options do we have when people are making fun of others' backgrounds?

THOUGHTS FOR STUDENTS

Burt's embarrassment about being Jewish, coming to the surface when threatened, is an example of how we all hide parts of ourselves from others when we feel threatened. So many of us hide parts of ourselves and/or our backgrounds for fear that we will be teased, physically harmed, and/or isolated. They were not the only ones that have done this in our country where being blond, thin, White, heterosexual, and blue-eyed was, and in many ways still is, considered the norm and by many, preferable.

African Americans have straightened their hair to "pass" as White. Chinese Americans make their eyes less slanted through plastic surgery. Jewish people have had nose jobs. Polish, Italian, Irish people, and so on have changed their last names to make them sound more "American." But, who can tell us what is American or is not? Who determines what kind of "look" is beautiful and what is not? Wouldn't it be nice if we could be confident that we wouldn't be picked on, teased, isolated, discriminated against for something that we are? Wouldn't it be healthier if we didn't have to carry a big bag of shame and embarrassment about ourselves, about things that we can't or don't want to change?

How can we do that? Well for one thing, it is important not to let the cultural stereotypes stereotype *you*. We live in a world of prepackaged images. We all know how some people sometimes look at us if we are a different nationality, sexual persuasion, color, or if we speak in a different language or have an accent. How often do we let those stereotypes embarrass us? How often do our parents or grandparents embarrass us because we feel they carry sides of ourselves we'd rather not let anyone see?

We often don't want to be associated with the stereotypes associated with those groups we are, nonetheless, part of. For me it was being Jewish and in the past I've reacted to various Jewish stereotypes—being cheap, stingy, and so on, by going to the extreme, by becoming overly generous and not at all concerned with matters of money. For some of you who are African American, Italian, Native American, gay, you know the stereotypes and I'm sure you've all tailored your behavior accordingly to make sure that no one can associate you with those attributes.

We should all strive to be proud of who we are and from where our ancestors have come. After all, our ancestors have given us the DNA or the building blocks for who we are and what we and our own descendants will be. They have given us our survival instincts and wisdom. We are also, and this is becoming more and more recognized, a stew of various traditions and cultures. For instance, let's consider someone who might be considered Italian:

Before there were Italians, there were villages and cities that had separate identities, like the island city of Venice and whose citizens considered themselves Venetian and not originally Italian and there were probably traders in Venice from the city we now call Tashkent in Uzbekistan; but in fact, in pre-Islamic and early Islamic times Tashkent was known as "Chach" and maybe a trader from "Chach" fell in love with someone from Venice and they had a child and that child was now considered a Venetian and maybe that child fell in love eventually with a Muslim trader from the Byzantine Empire, now Turkey, who was passing through Venice and they had a child and that child, when an adult, moved to Sicily, which was itself a mix of Germanic tribes, Catalonians (from what is now Spain) and Arabs or Moors, an unscientific term referring to a mixture of people—Berber, Black African, and Arab—and that now adult had moved from Venice, married a Sicilian and that child . . .

Anyway you get it. . . . This is what might be the very, very, very partial background of someone we call Italian. And the same complex mix of backgrounds is in all of us. Diversity lies within everyone! There is no such thing as "purity." We are all part of various cultures and traditions. Gender behavior or identification is also not "Black" or "White" and most of us, if we are willing to admit it, are a mix of the various stereotypes we associate with being male or female.

Interestingly, more and kids are taking pride in the fact that they are from "mixed parentage." Remember, there have always been kids of "mixed race" parents, but it had been, at least in my lifetime, hidden and/or stigmatized. Currently there is a lot more freedom to marry "outside" your self-identified racial or ethnic group and a lot more tolerance and appreciation for the children of those relationships. President Obama, who himself came from a marriage between a Kenyan and a Caucasian from Kansas, has led the way in this direction. In a country that had laws against Blacks and Whites marrying in certain states up through the 1950s, this is a really positive development. Children of these marriages have created organizations to support each other.

So, in some ways, when we make fun of someone for being one nationality or race, we are criticizing ourselves, because we are all sharing each other's DNA, as surely as we are breathing the same air. When we make fun of and stigmatize each other for being part of certain ethnic groups we are aligning ourselves with the worst aspects of our culture's history, one that has led to ethnic cleansing and extermination. Stereotypes lead to blaming, which can lead to anger, which can lead to violence.

At the same time when we use words of hate toward other groups, we are putting ourselves in a precarious position, because the ones on top could easily become the ones on the bottom and then how would you feel? The safest culture for anyone to live in is one where we celebrate each other's diversity, in background and in behavior. We often think in terms of either you're this or you're that, but in reality we have a great deal of everything inside us.

So, learn from the mistake Burt made and take pride in your heritage and in the mix that is "you." Celebrate the diversity both inside and outside of yourself and remember that there is no one way to be an American, except if being American means encouraging your own and each other's "pursuit of happiness" and sense of fulfillment.

THOUGHTS FOR TEACHERS

Curriculum and Pedagogical Suggestions: Immigrant History, Civil Rights, Global History, World Literature, and Biodiversity

How can you help your students feel pride in their backgrounds their own internal struggles?

For one thing, make sure that your school's literature and English curriculum reflect the diversity within our society.

- Does your curriculum include authors from various cultures and experiences? Are there books that tell the stories not only of White and Black people, but also of those from Asian and Middle Eastern backgrounds?
- Are there books written from a "mixed cultural" perspective in your library?
- Have you been able to locate books and films about people trying to "pass" between races, religions, nationalities, and sexual preferences? What have been the results of these attempts and how have they been portrayed?
- Are stories of gay and/or cross-gendered individuals available in your library or classroom?
- Do you have stories of immigrants and working people who have come to the United States?
- Are your stories about Native Americans filled with real and complex people, rather than romanticized stereotypes?

Educating students about the multiplicity of identities available to oneself and how people struggled to embrace the "glorious complexity" of their own identities is an important corrective to how previous generations portrayed seemingly impermeable "borders." Revealing the mutability of borders by studying the "real" lives of real people and the struggles many had in embracing their own diversity will help your students "own" and appreciate their own struggles to celebrate their own "glorious complexity."

American history has taught us so much about our "Founding White Fathers" that we often have much less time to talk about the history and contributions of others whose work was so essential to the construction of our nation. Remember, our country's wealth was largely accumulated through the work of slaves and immigrants and using land taken from the people native to our continent. We tell their stories far less than we tell the stories of the "Founding Fathers," "captains of industry," and "statesmen."

For instance, we often celebrate those who have "built" our great cultural and education institutions while ignoring how those "benefactors" made their money. This subsidiary role given to most people in the "story of America" can make it more difficult to embrace and honor our own backgrounds.

Most people in our country are not related to the wealthy few, but their ancestors' contributions to America are just as, if not more so, numerous and important. Most of our citizens are everyday people, struggling with making a living, working hard, paying bills. There is dignity in these efforts and this needs to be part of your curriculum so that their children can honor their ancestors and themselves, even if they are not part of a family tree that seems to get all the "sun and water."

How did and do films, TV, toys, video games, and music help create and perpetuate negative images of Latinos, Jews, African Americans, Native

Americans, gays, cross-gender individuals, and working people of all colors and nations? A really nice media awareness exercise is to study how various nationality and gender identity groups have been and still are being portrayed. How much of those stereotypes have been "picked up" and internalized by your students? Making these often invisible narratives visible helps them to challenge their assumptions about themselves and others.

The more you call your students' attention to the pool of stereotypes we are all immersed in, the more your students will be able to relax, accept, and celebrate their own and their classmates' heritage and diversity. Self-hating and hiding never produces the healthy, diversity-celebrating society we all want to be part of, one where we no longer have to be afraid just to "be."

Diversity itself needs to be understood as natural and as a gift. Ecological diversity is important for our species. Some plants protect others from disease and pests. Any species depends on the health of other species for their own health. A curriculum that teaches the role ecological diversity plays in the health of the "whole" will help students understand how the "weirdest"-seeming kids have a role to play in the health and intelligence of everyone. Recognizing how important diversity is for any ecosystem will help students understand that they too have contributions to make. Just as biodiversity is a measure of the health of an ecosystem, cultural, color, sexual, and gender diversity should just be not simply "accepted" or "tolerated," but encouraged and celebrated as beneficial to us all!

Chapter Three

The Storyteller's Vest

The land was hot, dry, and brown in Asha's village. On most days, howling winds would blow across the desert and its pale brown sand covered everything, even the insides of the small cobbler's shop where Asha learned from and worked with her father. Asha never liked the sand. It got into her hair and eyes and even after she washed, she still found it at night in her ears. Asha also never really liked to make shoes, but in her village, a boy follows her father's work like one camel follows anothis in the desert.

One afternoon when the sun was heavy and low on the horizon and the air hot and still and *nothing* in the world seemed new, a mustachioed man wearing a white turban and a grey and red shawl rode into the village atop a camel. He stopped at a small brown park where four roads came togethis and where the elders sat on benches talking and playing backgammon. From his bag, dusty with sand, the man took a long thin instrument and began to play. It sounded like two blades of grass blown between two thumbs.

Asha was one of many who were drawn to the park by the piercing tones. The stranger lit a lamp to hold back the darkness and unfurled a scroll. The scroll, red and black and gold, had pictures of birds, cows, trees, seas, kings and queens, soldiers and chariots painted upon it. As the stranger told stories, both he and the pictures came alive. He told stories of battles and of love and of people able to be human at one moment and gods at another. Asha, as were the others, sat hypnotized by the stranger's words that became magic carpets for their imaginations.

For Asha, however, the stories served a different purpose. They were not only wings for her imagination, but for her ambition as well. "Enough with shoes! I will become a storyteller!"

The day after the storyteller left the village, Asha left her father's shop as the sun was setting. she carried a goatskin drum to the park where the storyteller wove his spell the night before. Asha, a practiced drummer, began beating out a rhythm. To her surprise, the townspeople gathered around. Asha, like the stranger did the night before, lit a lamp and began retelling the stories the stranger had told. Her words, however, unlike the stranger's, came out haltingly, like rain squeezed from a desert sky. It wasn't long before most of his audience fell asleep or walked away. Asha was soon talking only to the stars except for one old man whose cane extended from his hand like a long finger.

"You know, Asha, if you really want to become a storyteller, I've been told that in the mountains there is a weaver who will make you a vest that will, when worn, bring words forth from your lips like water from a stream in the spring."

Those words were enough to give Asha the strength to finally leave her dry brown village. she knew that it was time to fulfill her destiny. Asha's journey into and through the mountains took him into lands filled with colors she hadn't known even existed; flowers that blazed with yellow, orange, and red; waterfalls where the water was green; and butterflies that were white and blue like clouds in the sky. The rivers sang and the leaves of plants were as broad as the roofs of houses.

Above the point where trees no longer grew, she saw a wooden hut, which clung to the side of a mountain. she walked closer when a voice from inside drew him closer.

"Come in," called a woman.

Asha walked cautiously through the door. The woman's hair was like white moss clinging to a stone and her red eyes shone like pieces of coal burning in an otherwise cold fire.

"So you want a storyteller's vest? Take this bucket," she said, extending the metal bucket with fingers like roots, "and fill it with gold. When you return, I will make you one. Make sure that you close the door on your way out. The wind blows cold into my house with no trees around to block its strength."

Asha took the bucket and walked back down the mountain, where she offered her services to anyone with gold to pay. she carried bags heavy as the world's sorrows, dug holes as deep as the unknowable, and cleaned more dirt than there was evil in the world. When her bucket was filled, she returned to the mountaintop and to the weaver and to the place where trees couldn't grow.

"Come in," said the weaver, knowing that Asha stood outside. She took the bucket and told Asha that she could stay in her barn while she worked on her vest, but never was she to come into her house while she was working.

Many days as the weaver worked, Asha spent her time tending to the old woman's garden and animals. Late at night while Asha sat outside the barn looking at the black, star-filled nights, she could see sparks of light leaping though the cabin's windows. she was tempted to come closer and look through the window to see the old woman work, but with her warning in her mind, she decided not to.

About the time of the year when pomegranates could first be harvested, the woman called for him into her house. "Here is your vest," the woman said. she had never seen anything like it. Surely the great sultans leading caravans through the desert never feasted their eyes on anything more magnificent.

The front of the vest was as blue as the sky and its back, as black as a moonless night. Threads of gold and silver delicately woven throughout the vest depicted all the animals known and imagined on the front, and the sun, the moon, and the sky's constellations shone from the back.

Asha put on the vest and as she did, she felt all the stories of the world ready to pour forth from her mouth like a river after the monsoons. The weaver's red eyes glowed. Asha thanked her as she walked from the wind-blown cliff.

At the first village she came to, Asha stopped at a park in its center. she beat her drum with the rhythm of the world's heartbeats, lit her lamp, and put on the vest and then began to tell stories that were surprising even to her. She told one about a serpent that grew wings to escape the heat of the ground and another about trees that could sing trouble to each other and another about cradles that soothed angry beasts and a dancer who danced so hard she could make storms and rain appear and of a painter who could color the sky. The stories glided off her tongue and lips and soon a large crowd formed. No sooner than one story stopped anothis began. The audience applauded so wildly it sounded like thunder and this time and each time after when she finished telling, the villagers threw him coins of gold and silver.

Her travels took her to places with animals so large they blocked the sun and people so small they could be mistaken for children, to places where men and woman danced the sun up, to places where the stars rested on top of children asleep in their beds. And as Asha told people her stories, the people who gathered, told him stories about *their* adventures, joys, and disappointments.

With some of the gold she received, Asha hired a young man to carry her coins, her lamp, her drum, and her vest. When they came to a village, Asha only had to clap her hands twice and reach back her arms and her vest would be placed on her shoulders. Words would come pouring out from her mouth and her audience would sit spellbound. Asha and her young assistant traveled throughout the kingdom, to places where wasps didn't sting and laughter was all the food people needed for their nourishment. From her sand-covered cobbler shop in that sand-covered village, Asha had come far as her fame, like the mushrooms, grew in the night after a healthy rain.

One day, the King and Queen summoned Asha. They asked her to tell stories at a party for the kingdom's royalty. Of course, she agreed. The night before her performance Asha made extra sure that her drum skin was tight, the lamp bright, and her vest as clean as it was when it came from the weaver's loom.

The King and the Queen greeted Asha warmly, telling her how excited they were to finally hear the famous teller of tales. Asha smiled proudly. she noticed how their dusty pink castle was a perfect backdrop for showing off the magnificent colors of the Queen's silk clothes that whispered when she walked. The walls of the castle were painted with pictures of the kingdom's history in turquoise and gold and the entryways of the building looked like entrances to dreams.

Asha was a bit nervous as she sat alone inside of thoughts, waiting behind the great dining room for her time to tell. When finally introduced by the King, nervousness left her body and she walked onto the stage with the confidence of a desert wind. Asha lit her lamp and played her drum, clapped twice and held out her arms, waiting for the vest . . . and she waited and she waited and she waited and no vest was placed on her back!

Asha turned to look for her assistant and looked then to the expectant audience. she realized that she had no choice but to speak. No words came out and her tongue felt as barren as a sand dune. All eyes stared at the storyteller and stuck her like daggers to her soul and confidence. At first the audience sat quietly, then they rustled uncomfortably and then, releasing their own tension, they began to laugh at the sight of the open-mouthed, silent storyteller. Asha, in a daze, walked from the stage and out the castle gates, silently meeting the desert and the dark night with her tortured mind.

Asha walked and walked and walked without gold and without stories. After many days in the desert she realized that she had no othis place to go but back to her sandy, dry village. When she arrived it was the first gray of early morning and the village looked even more barren than when she had left. The shops were still closed for the night and not a single owner was yet sweeping away the endlessly blowing sand from in front of their stores.

Asha went into her cobbler shop, looked around at what was still very familiar to her, wiped the sand from the tools, and workbench and began fixing the well-worn shoes that lay on the table from long ago. When the village woke up and morning activities began, word of Asha's arrival spread quickly. Everyone in the village came to the shop and gave their greetings, politely and discreetly. No one asked Asha why she had returned. They all knew that something terrible must have happened to bring this now famous storyteller back to her old and dry village and to the cobbler's bench that she had happily left so many years before.

Asha needed no time at all to remember the craft that had been her father's and grandfather's and soon the rhythm of village life became familiar as well: cleaning the shop at dawn, morning tea with the othis shopkeepers, conversations with her customers, the long lunches in the middle of the day, afternoon tea, the late afternoon sandstorm, cleaning the tools in the evening, closing the shop, the walk home past merchants selling their wares in the lamp-lit bazaar. There was, she was surprised to admit, a comfort to this predictability and familiarity.

One day, a young girl came into Asha's shop just as she was cleaning off her tools to end her day. The girl had dark brown skin and soft brown eyes, where curiosity and shyness met. "Excuse me," she said to Asha. "I have been told that you have traveled to places where sand is not the only thing one sees and where there are people you don't recognize. My friend tells me that all the villages in our kingdom look like ours and that there is no reason to travel anywhere. But I said that I didn't believe her and I know that there are great things to see and experience. Which is true?" In the young girl's eyes, Asha saw the hunger for adventure she had when she was her age.

"Tell your friend that you are the one who is correct. This kingdom is filled with places and people so different from here and so varied, your eyes and ears would need to be the size of boulders just to take in everything they could see and hear. I have seen mountains so tall that the sky begs them not to grow anymore. I have seen rushing waters that shone like jewels. I have seen birds with feathers the colors of the rainbow and I have spent time in the company of those whose customs were so new to me that my understanding stopped."

"Would you mind telling my friends ther?" the girl asked Asha.

"Bring your friends tomorrow at this time and I will tell them."

The young girl ran out of the cobbler's shop and the next day she came back with a few of her friends and Asha did as she had promised. she spoke about the lands she crossed and the people she met. The girls sat spellbound and told their friends about the joy and awe they received as they listened to Asha.

Each day, more and more people came as the cobbler cleaned the brown sand from her tools. They sat on stools and benches and squatted by the workbench listening to Asha tell about what she had seen on her travels: reptiles large enough to be ridden like camels, trees the size of hills. As they listened, they not only felt excitement for all that was new, but also as Asha talked of the people she had met and about their happiness, sadness, greed, and generosity, the villagers were reminded about their own dreams, hopes, and fears. Each evening, more and more people gathered at her shop until even people from nearby villages came to hear the cobbler, Asha, tell about her experiences.

For many years this tradition continued. Many who heard Asha's stories were inspired to travel. Many felt contentment from hearing these stories and returned happily to fulfill their domestic duties. Many planted gardens as the result of the beauty Asha described and many were inspired to look into themselves, where they felt what couldn't be seen or spoken of. Many were inspired to travel to rivers and oceans. All who came and listened sat on their own magic carpet that took them both away from and, at the same time, deeper into their villages and into the life they lived.

One evening as she closed her shop Asha paused to listen to the wind. she realized that she felt content, content to make and repair shoes and content to tell her stories to those who cared to listen.

As for the vest . . . As far as I know, it was never seen again. But, if you ever see someone wearing it, you might just be lucky enough hear a really good story, but then again, don't wait to see that vest to listen to a story and don't wait to wear that vest to tell your own. Remember, we all have stories to tell, even *you*.

QUESTIONS FOR STUDENTS

- Do you think that the vest was really magic? Why or why not?
- Did Asha think that there was magic in the vest? How can you tell?
- What made Asha finally feel content in her village?
- What kind of stories did Asha eventually tell that made her feel better?
- What kind of stories do you like to tell and when you do, how does it make you feel when you do?

THOUGHTS FOR STUDENTS

You are often told by grown-ups that your stories are unimportant. You aren't told this directly but you just kind of "understand it." When you speak about what you are doing and/or what you are thinking about, everyone is usually too busy to really listen. No one really asks too many questions and when you are finally listened to and you are speaking about what you are feeling or/and thinking about, you are told that you are being "cute" or too "dramatic." In school, while many writing prompts ask you to write about things you have experienced, the suggested topics are usually overly general and you often find it difficult to figure out what the prompt is after.

In this story, Asha's vest seems to be a solution for someone who has trouble even speaking, let alone telling a story. After the storyteller comes into her village, Asha realizes that she wants nothing more than to see that world and to tell stories. The stories coming from Asha's mouth once the vest is put on are indeed beautiful. However, without the security of the vest, no words emerge from the mouth of the by now famous storyteller. So, Asha goes back home, resuming a career she had left behind. It soon becomes clear that while the stories she had previously told are no longer available, instead, at the request of the young girl, she tells what he's seen and experienced, and that proves to be more than enough for him and for an audience that grows and grows.

We all need to understand that we have valuable things to say about what we've experienced and what we've thought about. While our lives will not necessarily be interesting to everybody, they need to be interesting to us. Inside of our stories are our lives. They contain experiences that made us happy and sad, things we were amazed by and things that bored us. To like our own stories is to like who we are. Often inside our stories are clues to who we are and who we want to be. Pay attention to your stories and to the stories of others. If you do, you will understand how we are uniquely "us" and also so similar to each other.

THOUGHTS FOR TEACHERS

Curriculum and Pedagogical Suggestions: Literacy

In this last story, while the tales that emerged from Asha's mouth once she put on the vest were indeed beautiful, the stories that emerged once she lost that vest and depended upon her experiences were just as beautiful and equally as compelling.

Encouraging your students to tell and honor their own stories helps them feel good about who they are. When you feel good about who you are, it is less likely you will harm another. By asking your students to tell their stories, the othis students will get to know who they are and from that knowledge empathy grows.

Create a classroom where personal stories are told and listened to and where students are trained to look for the big ideas and themes in a student's story. Do your students tell stories where she or he is always a victim? Do their stories end happily or tragically? Are their stories peopled by those who help or those who hinder? Are there heroic moments in their stories? Helping your students look at their own and other's stories in this way will help them notice the parallels between how they frame and tell their stories and how they live their lives. Do they perceive themselves as victims? Are their characters overwhelmed? Are they able to overcome adversity or are they overwhelmed by it?

Why?

Awareness of the patterns in one's stories is a good first step to "rewriting your script." Once your students become aware that, for instance, many of their stories they tell are tales of thwarted dreams, you can ask them both why their stories are organized in this way and whethis or not they feel they can rewrite them. Stories that leave characters powerless in the face of adversity and/or unable to overcome fears or negative behavior can be rewritten into those where agency is found. The more we are aware of how we frame the events of our lives, the more we have the power to rewrite them and to "shed skin" that limits us.

Chapter Four

Vengeance Highway

A Fast Road to Trouble

"Before you embark on a journey of revenge, dig two graves." —Confucius

When Peter's high school and track team friend, Bruce, got his first car it was at the end of his high school junior year. It was 1966, the time of "muscle cars" like the Oldsmobile 442 and the Plymouth Barracuda, sporty cars, like the Pontiac Firebird, the Mustang, and the Corvette, and luxury cars, like the Cadillac Eldorado. Gas was still cheap and the roads were new. But looking back on that now, there were small hints that maybe, just maybe, the time when we could build and clog up endless ribbons of roadways with cars going eight miles to a 30-cent gallon of gas, without any effect on our environment, might soon be coming to an end.

None of this affected Bruce, however, whose parents bought him the iconic muscle car of the times, a car that songs were written about. It was a brand new Pontiac GTO with an eight-cylinder engine and 400 ccu's, one the largest, fastest, and baddest autos around. Bruce first showed off his new car one day after track practice. His was a red convertible with white interior and it purred like a cat as it sat in front of the high school waiting for the guys on the track team to get in for their first spin. The GTO looked like a caged animal waiting to run. You could just about hear its breath.

After practice, Peter, Steve, Sean, and Jerry, who knew Bruce's car would be waiting for them, were still surprised when they saw it. They must have looked around, opened the hood, and looked under the car about ten times in envy and disbelief.

Bruce revved the engine. The guys got in and sunk down into what felt like custom-made seats and listened to a popular song from a British group called the Animals, "House of the Rising Sun."

Bruce drove slowly around the school in a very successful attempt to catch everyone's attention. With a button, Bruce took down the convertible top and smoothly drove once more around the school, again revving his engine, making the car growl. He took his track team friends to the back of the school where there was a straightaway along Grand Central Parkway and he drove faster and faster and faster, from 20 to 30, to 40 and 50, to 60 and 70 and 80. The speed pushed them back against their seats. In what seemed like a few seconds they were outside Pete's apartment

"Hey, let me out."

"What are you guys doing next Friday?" Bruce asked. "You want to go out to Long Island, or Long Beach? I want to see how fast I can take her on the highways."

For the next week or so, Bruce made sure that his GTO was always parked in the most visible spot in front of school, a spot where everyone could see as he waited for the track team to give them rides home. Each day, on the way home, he would take the guys to a hamburger place on Queens Boulevard called White Castle, that served small, really, really small hamburgers with onions, for a really small price. It was there that the guys on the team first understood that just like boys liked to meet girls, big muscle cars, like Bruce's GTO, liked to meet other cars and race with them.

Here's how it went: They'd eat their hamburgers in the White Castle parking lot with a whole fleet of other fast cars around them: 442s, Corvettes, Mustangs. Bruce would rev his car's engine and another car would answer back and it wasn't long before car followed car to the straightaway along Grand Central Parkway. They'd briefly park next to each other, rev their engines, and in a few seconds, both cars would be moving as fast as they could to a victory line, a line that both drivers seemed to know, yet was not obvious to the uninitiated.

On Friday night, Bruce picked Peter up at his apartment. The other guys were already in the car: Steve, Sean, and Jerry. They drove on roads that commuters took to get to work in New York City, that New Yorkers would take to visit their favorite beaches, and that families on Long Island used to come back to the "the island" on weekends after visiting grandparents who stayed in the "boroughs" rather than moving to the suburbs like their children.

Their first stop was a large restaurant called Nathan's; yes, the same Nathan's whose original shop was on Coney Island and that sold hot dogs, hamburgers, French fries, sodas, clams, and other foods that "required" the ketchup or mustard sloppily dispensed in various parts of the cavernous hall.

It was loud inside and around them were boys and girls about their age and a little older, talking, laughing, looking around.

The five of them went in a line that seemed to stretch back into Queens. As they stood for what felt like an endless amount of time, a short boy moved in front of them. Bruce tapped him on the shoulder and told him to get behind them. The kid ignored Bruce, and Bruce, a pretty big kid, picked the little guy up and lifted him out of the line. About seven kids, all older and larger than the any of those from the track team, came over and asked Bruce what he was doing, shoving everyone and Bruce. Afraid a losing fight was about to break out, Bruce, Pete, Steve, Sean, and Jerry left, without food, and ran toward Bruce's car with the older kids following.

They had been set up by an old trick: the smaller kid picked some sort of confrontation and when they responded, his bigger friends felt justified in retaliating. Luckily the kids from the track team beat the older kids to the GTO and quickly got in. Bruce started the engine, the wheels squealed, and the car jutted forward for the successful escape, driving eventually to a boardwalk not too far away.

They walked along the boardwalk trying to shake off the fear and humiliation that nested inside. The warmish spring night and the sound of the waves and some food from a boardwalk stand released the boys from whatever fear was still in their bodies and they were able to laugh and joke again. As they were leaving the boardwalk they saw that same little kid again, the one who had set them up, walking with one friend who looked like he was one of the boys who jumped them.

"Payback time," Bruce said.

"Five of us, two of them," Sean said. "Seems as fair as it was before."

"Nah, let's get back," said Jerry.

"One shot and we can go."

They surrounded the two boys who knew right away who their "would be" tormentors were and who encircled the two of them. Bruce went into the circle and slugged the little kid in the face. The little kid's friend stepped in and Steve jumped him from behind. Eventually, the track team guys left the two others on the boardwalk, not standing, but lying down, begging for mercy. Loudly and laughing, nervously with violence pulsing through their bodies like a drug, Bruce, Peter, Sean, Steve, and Jerry got back into the car full of conversations recalling their triumph.

"Did you see their faces when they saw us?"

"They weren't that tough when there were only two of them."

Bruce turned on the car and radio and drove to a gas station to fill up for the trip home. The neon lights lit the station like a movie set and a couple of cars were in the front and back of them. There was a car next to them, a beat-up '65 Plymouth Barracuda, a slick and pretty fast car with a V8. Pete noticed not only the car but who was in it.

"Hey, aren't those the guys from Nathan's?"

"There's that little kid too," said Peter.

All six boys in that car stared at the others in the GTO, while smiling demonic smiles, a smile that said, "Your time has come." They paid and Bruce peeled out, leaving the Barracuda in their dust. They whooped and hollered as they set out on their ride to the highway.

"The GTO smoked them," Sean said.

"Don't be so sure," said Peter. "They're right next to us!"

And indeed they were . . . not only next to the GTO, but they were moving their Barracuda closer and closer to its side. Bruce put the car into manual and shot past them, swerving in and out of the late night traffic with the Barracuda trailing close behind. Who knows what the other drivers on the highway were thinking; that these two muscle cars were competing against each other on a road probably filled with people coming home from dates or polite dinner parties. They must have been pretty scared with Bruce swerved back and forth along the highway, wheels squealing with each quick maneuver.

The Barracuda stayed close. Its driver moved his car closer and closer. Bruce had no way to maneuver. There were cars right ahead and right in back of him and he couldn't find a way through. The other car began hitting the side of the GTO. This made Bruce crazy. The Barracuda slammed against them with even more force.

Bang! Bang! Bang!

They heard a piece of Bruce's car fall off loudly onto the highway.

Bang! Bang! Bang!

The look in the eyes of those kids got crazier and crazier as they savored their revenge.

Bruce opened up the window and threw out an equally maniacal look and said, "OK you asked for it."

"Bruce," Peter said, "let's just go. It's over."

"Not a chance!"

"Let it go," Steve yelled.

Suddenly, Bruce turned the steering wheel to the left and he banged into the Barracuda and forced it off the road. It swerved and swerved and swerved, until tipping over onto the grass by the side of the road, looking like a turtle on its back.

"Yes!" Bruce shouted, raising his hands in the air. But as he did, the GTO escaped from his control and now they too were cascading off the road and toward the grass. Bruce tried to get his big car under control, but it was too late and the car, by now, had a mind of its own. The next thing the guys knew was that the car had come to a stop.

Pete looked around the car and heard groaning and moaning and felt another leg on top of his. Then came the police sirens. It took the police and ambulance about thirty minutes to get all the boys out of the car and into an ambulance and another thirty after that to be wheeled into a nearby hospital's emergency room. They gave the cops their names and phone numbers and not long afterward, parents came.

The whole scene was a mess, with questions from parents and police coming like bullets from a machine gun. Luckily and probably miraculously, no one was seriously injured. Steve had a broken arm as did Bruce. Peter had a neck brace. Sean and Jerry had broken legs and bandages on their head.

A couple hours later, Peter walked out of the hospital with his parents. He noticed one of the kids who had been chasing them. He was walking out with his parents as well. The kid no longer looked maniacal. He was a just a regular teenager, confused, dazed, and trying to come to terms with what had happened, while recovering from the shock of the accident and the pain in his body.

Their eyes caught each other's.

He started to speak first.

"You OK?" he asked

"Yea, a few broken bones, I guess. You?"

"We're OK. Close call. One of us is in the operating room for some stuff that was damaged inside his body . . . spleen or something I think. They say he's OK."

"Good," Pete said.

He nodded. "We got off lucky, huh?"

"Yeah."

"See ya," he said.

"Yeah."

QUESTIONS FOR STUDENTS

- Whose fault was the accident? Why?
- Have you ever tried to get revenge on someone? Was it successful? Why or why not? What would having success have meant in this regard?
- Can you imagine another way to have reacted? What?
- Do you agree with the Confucius quote at the beginning of the story? Why or why not? What does it mean to you?
- Even though the passengers weren't driving Bruce's car, were they responsible for what happened as well? Why or why not?
- Was there a moment in the story when the boys could have just left and gone safely home?
- What did all of them gain from their actions? What did they lose?

THOUGHTS FOR STUDENTS

Seeking revenge is an old, old strategy, one that individuals as well as nations have used. You do something to me, I'll do something to you. The underlying thought is that the potential for revenge keeps everyone in check.

In what was called the Cold War, between around 1946 to 1989, the United States and the Soviet Union were constantly competing against each other and the threat of violence loomed over these two countries. Each increased its military budget and the number of nuclear weapons it had. This strategy was called "mutual deterrence." It simply meant that if you knew I had nuclear bombs and I knew that you had nuclear bombs, we would be afraid to start a war because the potential for "mutual retaliation," payback or revenge, would hover over both countries.

This seemed to work. No one was actually bombed by the other country. But if you look at the results of the Cold War more closely, you'll see how the Cold War hurt other countries who were "friends" with the bigger ones. Money that could have been used to help US and Soviet citizens live more prosperous, healthy, and happy lives was used to prop up military budgets and smaller countries, who were caught in the crossfire, were invaded, bombed, and had their governments taken over by people who liked one or the other of the big countries.

A strategy where the potential for vengeance was always floating over these two giant countries left each country and the rest of the world perpetually nervous while the big countries kept playing a game of "one-upmanship," as the "stakes" were continually raised.

The same was obviously true for those kids who were in the "muscle cars" that night. It was like that poker game where instead of "holding" they kept "raising the stakes" until both groups were "broke" from the "bets" they made. The accident demonstrated that there is never a "winner" in a game of revenge. When does it stop? When is it "over"? Never! Once in a game whose point is to constantly seek revenge, there is no way it could ever end, except through a crash, an injury, or death.

No one is ever a winner, even though we all imagine we can be the one who does win. Ask yourself when you are seeking "payback" just what you really want. Wouldn't you simply like to go about your business and feel good? How does revenge bring you closer to that goal? How does the momentary success, measured by your "boys" slapping you on your back, help you get to your ultimate goals in life? What are you after, your friends' momentary "respect" or your health, safety, and a future that is not dependent on having to worry about who is disrespecting whom?

Payback might seem sweet, but it is a "fool's gold," a false promise that quickly leaves you with a bad taste in your mouth and no food for your soul. It promises one thing and delivers another, like a big fluffy cone of cotton candy. Keep your balance. Think of what game you are playing. Again, ask yourself what your ultimate goal is and whether revenge is the best way to get you there, or, more likely, a detour that might end up in a dead end.

THOUGHTS FOR TEACHERS

Curriculum and Pedagogical Suggestions: Social Studies and Global Studies

Revenge is all too often the justification for why both students and adults act toward each other in the way they do. I'm sure that you've heard it: "He or she 'dissed me!' Nations are not any different. They seek revenge on one another. Just look at the American invasion of Iraq after 9/11, when its justification was revenge for the bombing of the World Trade Center (even though it was clear that Iraq had nothing to do with it).

Revenge has been an important component in literature as well. For instance, in Shakespeare's *Hamlet* , revenge is very present as a man avenges the murder of his father by killing his uncle. Also, check out Homer's *The Iliad* for some intense examples of revenge. The scapegoating of others, a cousin of revenge, has often been used to justify heinous acts of revenge, like in 1930s and 1940s Germany—"The Jews caused our economic problems, so . . ."

On one hand there seems to be something so "correct" about revenge. After all, someone does something to you and you do something back. It almost seems that it is balancing the universe, "tit for tat." After all, isn't the phrase "An eye for an eye" a G-d-given directive to seek and receive revenge? Truth be told, this biblical phrase's meaning is open to question. Some say that in biblical times, punishment for past deeds was often way out of proportion to the crime and that the admonition "An eye for an eye" should be read as "*Just* an eye for an eye."

In addition to using history and literature, there is another curriculum area that can be used to stimulate conversation about revenge. Notice how the justice system works in various societies. What is society's role toward those who have transgressed its identified boundaries? Should it jail the transgressor, banish them to a lifetime of isolation in the jungle, or on an ice floe, work toward rehabilitation? Ask the Innocence Project, a group dedicated to the use of DNA to free the innocent prisoners, how many falsely accused citizens ended up spending large swaths of their lives in prison, on death row, or even executed. Is this an example of "revenge gone wild"?

How should we, as a people, individually and collectively, guard against false accusations and the false rewards of retaliation? Has revenge ever been justified? What are its consequences? Does it get us what we are after?

Helping your students identify and interview adults or older teenagers who acted from revenge and retaliation, only to experience its severe consequences, would be a good exercise and a good place to start "reprogramming" your students' understanding of the effectiveness, or not, of revenge-based justice. This is another way to help your students realize that retaliatory behavior, while appearing to be righteous and correct, actually puts the "revenger" in a worse position than before their desire for revenge was acted upon.

Help your students ask themselves what they want from life and what they feel is the best way they can get there. There are very few answers to this question that would include the possible physical and legal consequences connected with retaliatory behavior.

Lastly, ask your students how they feel about Gandhi's famous aphorism about revenge, "An eye for an eye will only make the whole world blind."

Chapter Five

A Neighbor's Secret

I grew up in an apartment building, a six-floor apartment building, set amid a forest of six-floor apartment buildings in what was called the "Bedroom Borough" of Queens, New York City. Imagine all those apartments, each filled with people with their loves, resentments, hopes, and dreams. Each apartment filled with cooking smells, an occasional cat or dog, just-married sons or daughters, just-born children, and/or just–passed away parents, grandparents, friends.

This was my childhood . . . caves of apartments, each containing a library of stories, but to tell you the truth, the other side of the coin was that you really didn't know most of the stories behind the doors. Folks in the 1950s and 1960s, at least where I lived, pretty much kept to themselves. They went about their business, as far as I could see, behind their locked doors.

As kids, or course, we got into other apartments more often than our parents did. There were the friends you visited, some occasionally and some nearly every day. You walked in, said hello to parents and siblings, and then went into your friend's room to play, oblivious to anyone else's life. There was, of course, Halloween, when you knocked on doors and were received by those you only vaguely knew and who had candy in their hands.

We had only three neighbors in the apartment next door to ours during the almost sixty years my father and mother lived in our two-bedroom, two-bathroom apartment. They were the Weisses, the Cohens . . . and then, there was Mrs. Susman.

Mrs. Susman was a woman my mother's age. She, like my mother, was perfectly and neatly dressed and her hair was always without a wild or unruly strand. She had a soft, sweet smile and, like my mother, was very quiet. Her relationship with my mother was friendly, polite, and shy at the same time. Small hellos, a simple chat by their mutual doors, and later, gaining more intimacy, a ring of our doorbell by Mrs. Susman and a much longer conversation in the hall. Never in my memory was the sanctity of their mutual apartments broached . . . never was anyone invited in for tea or coffee. It didn't seem to matter to either, however. Their hall meetings were all that each needed, a little companionship with an equally intelligence- and privacy-respecting person.

One day, having come from my Rhode Island home to New York City to visit my mother and father I noticed Mrs. Susman in the hall. I said hello and she told me how nice it was that I continued to regularly come "home" to help take care of my mother and father, both of whom had Parkinson's disease. She said in her Old World of Poland, they said that those who take care of their parents would be blessed. Later during this particular visit, while we were waiting for the elevator, she seemed to feel the urge to speak to me. I listened and the conversation continued even as the elevator came and went a number of times. Here is her story, one story of many, usually held tightly within the confines of our separate apartments, but this time, shared.

> I was born in a small village in Poland, in a house with my father, mother, and two sisters. My father was a tailor and my mother worked inside the house doing housework and a little sewing for the neighbors. I was the studious one in my family. I read anything I could get my hands on . . . novels, poetry, history books. I did well in school and was allowed to go to Warsaw to attend college. While there were rumblings against Jews back in the 1930s, it wasn't until 1939 when I realized that there might be real trouble for my people.
>
> The Germans who had invaded my country began to round us up and put us into overcrowded ghettos. I was called into the president's office at my college and told that I would no longer be permitted to study at the university because I was Jewish. I packed my belongings and went back to my village. Once off the bus and home it was clear to me that our situation had changed for the worse.
>
> Some Jewish people whom I recognized were now wearing large Jewish stars pinned to their clothing and some were being rounded up from their homes and being led toward the train station. When I arrived at my parents' house, no one was home. All the lunch dishes were still on the table and the coffee filled the cups. The house reminded me of the stories I had read about the day the volcano erupted in Pompeii, where the lava flowed over the houses and people and daily lives were stopped in the middle of everyday life. I went through the house to see if by some miracle any of my family was still around.
>
> I looked into the various rooms, desperate to find someone, my grandmother, mother, father, one of my two brothers, or maybe my uncle, aunt, or cousins who lived down the street and who often came over for lunch. But there was no miracle and instead I saw overturned bureaus and drawers with their content sprawled over the floors and bed, jewelry boxes rummaged and pictures removed from their frames, all indications that people, maybe the police, the army, local citizens had searched for valuables.

Suddenly I heard someone coming through the front door and immediately thought that it was the police returning to see if they had missed anyone or anything. I hid under one of the beds and surprisingly heard a familiar voice calling my name. It was Mrs. Slotski, our neighbor. Mrs. Slotski was a nurse at a local hospital and was always kindly polite and somewhat distant. She and her husband were Catholic and would walk to church together every Sunday until a few years before when her husband passed away.

"Sophia," she called. "Sophia!"

When I came out from under that bed and went into the hall, she grabbed me and pulled me to her and cried. I began to cry as well.

"They came." That is all she said but I knew what she meant.

"You must not stay in here. They will come back to see what they missed."

"Where am I to go?"

"You will come and into my basement and you'll stay there."

I collected a few pieces of clothing hurriedly and walked outside briefly where I saw a sign that said it was illegal to shelter Jews, to give them or to sell them food. To do so, the sign continued, would result in the punishment of death.

So my life changed once again. I stayed almost four years in the basement of that house and during the entire time Mr. Slotski would bring me my meals, change the bedsheets and do my laundry, and bring books to read, a radio to listen to, and water for washing. I dared never to leave my basement. Sometimes Mrs. Slotski would come down and play cards with me and talk about who was and wasn't still in our neighborhood. She maintained her polite distance, but her actions demonstrated closeness and a commitment to keep me safe. Remember, all this occurred with the backdrop of possible imprisonment and/or death for both of us.

Sometimes I heard visitors upstairs. One spoke German and from the heavy sound of his boots, he sounded like someone in the army. I remember that when he came over I would smell special foods upstairs and soft and romantic music swirled around above me and the shuffling of shoes made me feel that the two were dancing. The German came more and more often and I realized that Mrs. Slotski must have had a German soldier for a boyfriend. After he left, Mrs. Slotski would bring down to me what remained of the day's special foods.

Then, one day, I heard bombs and a lot of commotion in the street. It sounded like tanks and gun and people scurrying. I turned on the radio. The Russians were advancing into Poland. From above, I heard the front door slam open and in Russian, a language I understood, I heard a man scream, "*Sotrudnichal s vragom!*" and again, "*Sotrudnichal s vragom!* [Collaborator!]" and Mrs. Slotski kept screaming "*Niet, niet . . .* ["No . . ."]" The yelling stopped and I heard Mrs. Slotski being led outside.

For the first time in four years, I climbed the stairs, opened the door to the basement slightly, just in time to watch Mrs. Slotski being led away and out into the street. Cautiously I went to the window. The Russian tanks, looking like water buffalo at a watering hole, were everywhere and the neighbors were out taunting Mrs. Slotski, in Polish, "*Renegat, Renegat*" . . . "Traitor, Traitor."

I understood that my situation had changed again and I no longer had to hide. It was difficult to believe at first. During the first two days I stayed upstairs, but hid in the basement at night. On the third day, when there was a knock at the door, I hid. I noticed two Polish policemen, one of whom I had known from schooldays. I decided to let them know I was there. The two jumped when I made my presence known. Anton was the boy I knew.

"What are you doing here, Sophia?" he asked.

"What happened to Mrs. Slotski?" was all I could say.

The two looked at each other and spit on the ground.

"She was a collaborator, a traitor. She had a German officer as a boyfriend. Who knows what she told them about us."

"Where is she now?"

"She has been taken to prison and will be put on trial and will no doubt be killed."

Those words sent a chill through my body.

"But she saved my life."

"What?"

I told them the story of how Mrs. Slotski had saved my life and protected me throughout the war. They, in turn, told me where she was being held at the police station. Immediately I went into the street for the first time in four years. My town was mostly rubble. I saw faces I knew, but they were now older, sadder, and cautious. There were also the victorious Russian soldiers who directed traffic, sat by tanks, and looked confident. None of those I saw, as far as I knew, were Jews.

Inside the police station I told my story and waited. A man in a tattered police uniform emerged from an office in the back. I knew him from before the war. He looked much older than I had remembered him.

"Miss Grossman, I understand that you have something to tell us about the collaborator, Mrs. Slotski."

I told him and left. He listened, but said nothing.

I was not sure where to go. Many in the street were busy fixing up their houses damaged by the war. I walked past my family's house and knocked on the door. Another family, whom I didn't know, was living there. I went back to Mrs. Slotski's house.

A few days later, the police came to the house again and told me that Mrs. Slotski would not be killed thanks to my testimony. She would be kept in jail for a few months and would give testimony against her wartime boyfriend and would then be released. He told me about a place I could go where Jews could learn about the fate of their relatives who were missing.

The next day, I went there. Up on the walls were notes from those who were trying to find loved ones. I looked for those from members of my family. There were none there. I met with an administrator who checked on my family. He told me he needed some time to research where they were. I returned in a couple of days and was told that all had been taken to Auschwitz and murdered.

One month later, I met a man who too had lost his family. We fell in love, got married, and we moved to the Bronx soon after. He died after thirty years of marriage. We had a son. After my husband died, I moved here, next to your parents.

Last month, I received a phone call. It was from Mrs. Slotski. She had gotten my phone number through some people who had moved to Israel after the war. They had recently returned to our town on a visit where they met Mrs. Slotski, who asked about me. Luckily, those people knew how to reach me. So, Mrs. Slotski will come to the United States next month and we will tour the United States to speak about our friendship that saved both of our lives.

"Now you know," she said.

Mrs. Susman smiled and went into her apartment.

QUESTIONS FOR STUDENTS

- Why do you think Mrs. Slotski risked her life to save my neighbor's life?
- Do you think she was scared and if so, how did she overcome her fear?
- Have you ever stood up for somebody who was being picked on or teased?
- If yes, how did it feel and if not, how did it feel?
- If you were scared to help, why?
- If you did help, were you scared at first and if so, how did you overcome your fear?
- Which do you think is worse, bullying someone or watching someone be bullied and not doing anything about it? Why?

THOUGHTS FOR STUDENTS

I was always surprised, after Mrs. Susman shared her story, that in spite of all the tragedy she had experienced, how happy and contented she seemed. Perhaps it was because in spite of all she had suffered, she had experienced an amazing example of self-sacrifice and kindness and secondly, she had been able to pay back the person who saved her life. I'm sure that there were other reasons as well, including having a good marriage, a nice son, a loving childhood, but I'm also sure that the acts of kindness and heroism on her behalf and her own contribution to "good" in the world made her feel that in the midst of one of the worst periods in human history, all was not lost.

Later in life, while in India, I ran across a very happy younger woman. She was living in the United States but was originally from Holland. She told me that both sets of her grandparents hid Jews in the war at risk of their own lives and the lives of their families.

I wonder what makes someone do this, to stand up for somebody, to protect somebody, even at the risk of their own and often their immediate family's well-being? What is it about human beings that allows some of them to put their own health and safety second and another's, first? So much on TV and in the films shows people plotting against each other and yet in our lives and in the lives of others, there have been equally if not more examples of people being kind to one another.

These non-Jewish people who hid Jewish people and/or helped them escape from the Nazis are called "Righteous Gentiles" and many of their stories are online and at the Holocaust Museums in Washington, DC, and Israel. But remember, they aren't the only ones who have risked harm or scorn for their action in support of others.

The baseball shortstop named Pee Wee Reese was a star for the Brooklyn Dodgers when Jackie Robinson, the first African American to play in the major leagues, came up from the minors to the Dodgers. In the spring of 1947, when Robinson came to the Dodgers for the first time, many on that team were not happy about an African American integrating their team, and a petition circulated saying that they wouldn't play if Robinson was allowed to. Reese, who was the captain of the Dodgers and a southerner as well, refused to sign it.

History is filled with people who didn't stand by and watch someone being injured through teasing or physical actions. Jews were hidden in mosques and churches during World War II. African Americans have protected Whites in racial riots. Whites have set up safe houses for runaway slaves, and boys and girls like you have refused to have boys and girls in their school become the objects of bullying, teasing, gossiping, or isolation.

We've all been on both sides, sometimes standing up and telling a kid not to bully another and sometimes letting it happen. I have had others stand up and say something when I was being bullied and had people stand by or even join in when I was being teased. To get involved and risk teasing or worse, the punches of others, is scary. But the truth is, everyone who steps in to help another is probably scared.

Becoming a hero doesn't mean that you are not scared, only that you acted despite your fear. Standing by and not doing anything means you accept bullying and teasing as part of your life and by being an audience to it, you tell the world that it is OK to do it. Bullies need an audience as surely as actors do and as surely as fire needs air.

A little while ago, an old friend from elementary school saw another boy who was not really a friend of ours, but was in our class. My friend told the other boy (now a doctor) that he was in touch with me. The doctor smiled and said that he remembered that I would always include him in games when no one else wanted to. It made me feel good to hear that. At the same time, I remember being part of a group, in fact the instigator of the group, who taunted a girl in junior high. I still carry guilt for that.

Why did I help one kid and not the other? I don't know why, but I can tell you that it certainly made me feel better knowing I had a positive effect on another's life and that he remembered it almost forty years later. Standing by as bad things happen to others goes against our better selves. We understand and when we feel another's pain and do nothing to lessen that pain, we feel it in ourselves. It is a betrayal of who we are.

These Righteous Gentiles, Pee Wee Reese, and many others through history in small and large ways created for themselves and others the kind of life they wanted to live and the kind of world they wanted to be part of. Built into all of us is the desire to help one another. We feel each other's pain and we can feel another's pain as our own. To act upon this empathy, at the risk of your own comfort, is not easy, which is why it is heroic.

Mrs. Slotski was a hero and I hope that she can be a model for you, when you and your friends are watching a bully push someone, tease someone, gossip about someone, isolate someone. And remember, it is not just heroic to get involved, it is also smart, because one, it will make you feel better and stronger and two, the world you create will be the one you live in.

THOUGHTS FOR TEACHERS

Curriculum and Pedagogical Suggestions: US and Global History, Holocaust Studies, Civil Rights

Heroic figures who risked their own and their family's health and safety to protect others don't receive the kind of attention in schools they deserve. How else can our students find role models to help them overcome their fears about "sticking up" for each other?

One of Israel's Yad Vashem Holocaust Museum's tasks is to honor non-Jews who risked their lives, liberty, or positions to save Jews during the Holocaust. The Righteous receive a certificate of honor and a medal and their names are commemorated in the Garden of the Righteous Among the Nations, on the Mount of Remembrance, Yad Vashem. As of 2008, more than 23,000 individuals have been recognized as "Righteous Among the Nations."

It is important when reading about these people or if you are lucky, to be able to bring them into class, that you make sure that your students understand how those who helped others, they dealt with their own fear (www.gariwo.net/eng_new/foreste/yadvashem.php). Why? Too often these and other heroes are portrayed as people without the fear any of us would feel were we in their place and therefore impossible to emulate. Your students need to understand that those who came to the aid of others had fear like anyone else, but acted heroically anyway.

Here are some other events you might ask your students to research and then to use in their discussion about "Why do people help?"

• Biographies of Jackie Robinson and Pee Wee Reese
• Stories of the Underground Railroad
• Learn about the Innocence Project and the lawyers who help inmates on death row gain their innocence using DNA tests

- Stories about the people who took part in Freedom Summer (http://
  en.wikipedia.org/wiki/Freedom_Summer) including James Chaney (a
  Black CORE activist from Mississippi), CORE organizer Michael
  Schwerner, and summer volunteer Andrew Goodman (both of whom were
  Jews from New York) who were murdered that summer for their work
  with the project
- Biographies about Gandhi and those who participated in the nonviolent
  efforts of freeing India from British rule
- Learn about the Anti-Apartheid Movement
- Find, if you can, people who lived in South Africa, the American South,
  and/or Nazi-ruled Germany who didn't get involved while others were
  suffering. Ask them to speak about how they feel about their decision now
- Talk about how you and others you know did or didn't get involved in
  helping another in need and how it made you feel about your decision now
- Brainstorm with your students about what would help them be more involved when they are witness to bullying, teasing, isolating types of behavior.

There are many, many other stories about those who took a risk to help
others. It still happens every day; antiwar protestors, soldiers who rush into
the line of fire to save another, Greenpeace activists, police and firemen who
charge into dangerous situations, the first responders at Ground Zero on 9/11,
whistleblowers, and so forth.

There are just as many, if not more, heroes than villains. We just don't
hear about them and we should! One of my favorite books on this subject is
Rebecca Solnit's *A Paradise Built in Hell*. In it she speaks about our twentieth-century human and natural disasters and how, after they occurred, citizens got together to form "communities of caring." Check out this book and
see what stories would be appropriate for your students to demonstrate how
caring we can all be.

Chapter Six

A New Student Stops Their World

She came into their classroom like a tornado blowing through a midwestern prairie. She had a tight miniskirt, her hair up like cotton candy at a county fair, and bubble gum snapping in her mouth like a whip. She had long eyelashes and dark purple eye shadow and a sneer that would have made the devil back down. She was Agafya Orphanides, new kid in school. She came into sixth grade like a typhoon into a village made of playing cards.

The principal brought her into class for the first time. Mr. Tauchner, the same man who each year would give out report cards and each year, say to most of the students, "You can do better." Mr. Tauchner whispered into their sixth-grade teacher Mr. White's ear, smiled at them, and left. Mr. White was just that, White. Everything about him was white: white shirt, white skin, white hair, white mustache. His sports jacket looked newly bought, his Windsor knot tied like that of the king of England's butler's, and the creases of his pants could cut a steak. His back was straight and his desk ordered. As he introduced Agafya Orphanides, it was immediately clear that this was not a match made in heaven.

Mr. White reluctantly and with some embarrassment introduced Agafya to our class. The boys were understandably fascinated by this girl who was obviously from another much more "advanced" world. The girls were equally fascinated, but with a mix of apprehension and jealousy. You see, mostly they, the kids in class, were a pretty compliant bunch, completing work on time, coming in with clothes that would be acceptable anywhere and for any occasion, and never, or hardly ever, doing anything that would stand out. So, when miniskirted, gum-snapping Agafya stood before them with hair up like an angry shout, it was as if someone from another world stepped into theirs.

Agafya smiled at the students and she popped her gum at the same moment she was introduced by Mr. White.

"Miss Orphanides," said Mr. White, "we don't chew gum in class. Please put it in some paper and throw it in the garbage." Agafya popped it once more, took a piece of paper off Kenny Blair's front row desk, wrapped up the chewy wad, and threw it into the garbage can and then strutted back to an empty desk at the end of a row of desks.

Mr. White began his lecture.

"So, what were we studying about before our new student came in?"

Still recovering from the tornado that blew into our room, no one raised their hands.

"I repeat, what were we studying about before Mr. Tauchner brought Miss Orphanides into the room?"

One tentative hand rose. It was Reggie Sanderson, who could always be counted on to butter up a teacher any chance he had.

"We were studying about explorers," he said.

"That's right," said Mr. White. "And what explorers are we currently studying?"

"Christopher Columbus," answered Howard.

"Good. And what do we know about Christopher Columbus?"

"That he discovered America," answered Reggie.

Agafya's arm shot up.

"Yes, Miss Orphanides?" Mr. White said.

"Well, technically, Chris didn't discover America. After all, weren't there American Indians already there?"

"Yes, of course."

"So, how did he 'discover' America when there were already people?"

"Yes, very good, Miss Orphanides. OK. Let's go on, shall we? So, Reginald, what was the reaction of Europe when Columbus came back?"

"They were very surprised, sir, because everyone thought that he would fall off the flat earth."

"Very good, Mr. Sanderson."

"That's not really true, sir," Agafya blurted out. "Many people realized that the earth was not flat by that time. Actually, everyone was kind of disappointed when Chris came back because he didn't bring any gold, like he promised."

"Miss Orphanides, in this class we raise our hands."

Agafya decided to keep quiet after that, not compliantly, but with the most antagonistically looking physical posture style anyone in the class had ever seen. Her legs stretched out into the aisle and her head back as if she were leaning on an invisible pillow. She just sat there, and dared Mr. White to say something.

Mr. White continued his lecture on explorers until the bell rang and the class went to lunch. The buzz was definitely Agafya, who, with great confidence, went into the back of the cafeteria, sat by herself, and took out the strangest lunch anyone had ever seen. It was not a sandwich; it came out of a metal container. Whatever she ate was sort of rectangular and white.

The others at the table where Jimmy, David, Richard, Kenny, and Brian ate looked at Agafya's lunch and wondered what it was that she took out of her brown bag. They dared each other to go ask her and finally, Brian agreed.

"Excuse me, the others at my table were wondering what you are eating?"

"Then why don't you sit down and ask me?"

Flustered by her directness, Brian sat down.

"Now try first saying 'Hello' and telling me your name."

"Brian."

"Good. Your question . . . ?"

"Well some of the guys over there were wondering what it is you are eating. It doesn't seem like a sandwich."

"First, I find it interesting that a bunch of guys would care about what I was eating. Second, it really is none of your business. Third . . . it's tofu. What is tofu, you are, I'm sure, asking yourself. It is made of soybeans. They eat it a lot in Japan and China. "

"Why would you eat that?"

"Because, I need to get protein."

"Doesn't meat have protein?"

"I'm a veg."

"What?"

"I'm a vegetarian. I don't eat meat. Killing animals for food is barbaric."

"You don't eat meat? Are you kidding?"

"No."

"Why?"

"I already told you . . . I wouldn't kill something just so that I could survive."

"But you don't actually 'kill' it."

"True, but you are part of the system that kills, if you agree to eat dead animals. After all, weren't all Germans responsible for the Holocaust?"

"Eating meat is like the Holocaust?"

"Not the same. I was merely pointing out that whatever one does, we must take responsibility for our actions and inactions."

"You are weird."

"Thank you, Brian. Now you can go back to your friends and tell them how weird I am and talk about the latest baseball results. That is what you guys like to talk about, isn't it?"

"Very weird."

"Good-bye Brian, so nice to talk with you," she said sarcastically.

He walked back to his friends.

"So, what was it?" David asked.

"Tofu."

"What?"

"Tofu. Tofu. Tofu. It's made from soybeans and they eat it in China or Japan, or somewhere. I can't believe you don't know what tofu is!"

"OK, OK. Sure I know it. By the way, Koufax is pitching tonight."

Brian had never met anyone like Agafya and of course, neither had anyone in school, including Mr. White. Each day she'd come in wearing something unique . . . a bright gold and silver scarf, a black beret with red stars, glass bracelets that clanked together when she walked, black stockings, or a colorful poncho that she proudly announced came from Mexico when Howard got the nerve up to ask where it was from and what it was. There had never ever been anyone like her. Never!

Some of the girls befriended her. Susan and Vicky invited her to their houses. But neither of them would tell the others about Agafya's apartment. It was as if they had gone into some kind of sorcerer's cave and to reveal its contents would inflict you with fifty years of bad luck. It wasn't long before a few of the girls were even wearing black stockings like Agafya's and putting on purple eye shadow on their way to school. As for Mr. White, he couldn't have been less happy. He hardly got through any lesson without Agafya's interruption.

For instance, one day when they were studying poetry and Mr. White began talking about people like Lord Byron, Shakespeare, Keats, and Shelley, Agafya just shouted out, "I saw the best minds of my generation . . ."

"What was that?"

"I saw the best minds of my generation. That's the first line of Allen Ginsberg's poem 'Howl.' You know who Allen Ginsberg is, don't you, Mr. White?"

"I believe I've heard of him, yes. Not a real poet, but a beatnik." Beatniks were the "nonconformists" of the time, known, at least in the media for their berets, their poetry, their jazz, and their lack of interest in "work." A "beatnik" on the TV show *The Many Loves of Dobie Gillis* always was scared when someone mentioned "work."

"How can you say he's 'not a real poet,' Mr. White? He is changing the way people write poetry, just as surely as Walt Whitman changed the way poetry was written a hundred years before."

"It remains to be seen, young lady, whether or not your Mr. Ginsberg will have a fraction of the effect on world poetry as Shelley or Keats."

"He already has, Mr. White. When I go down to Greenwich Village, there are hundreds of young people all reciting poetry like Allen Ginsberg. "

"Mimicking the rhymeless, rhythmless squawking of Mr. Ginsberg is not an example of long-term staying power. We need a good hundred years to assess the effects of an artist on our culture. Your beatniks of Greenwich Village could be and I dare say, might be destroyers of all that is good in our culture, with their filthy hair, beards, and black turtlenecks."

"That's not true. Jack Kerouac and Allen Ginsberg love America. It is just a different America that they love. I just would like to know why we can't read something written now and not in some sort of moldy past?"

"That's enough, Miss Orphanides, but I do thank you for your astute observations and contribution."

Or the time when Mr. White was discussing the Civil War and Agafya blurted out, "There still is slavery."

"How do you mean that, Miss Orphanides?"

"Well not actual slavery, but racism. Look at the South, separate drinking fountains, sections of buses, fewer opportunities for jobs. It might not be slavery, but it certainly is related."

"Miss Orphanides, please keep your terms straight. Slavery is one thing. The residue of segregation is another. Besides, the South is making great strides."

"Great strides? Great strides? Did you see how many lunch counters, swimming pools, and clubs are still closed to Negroes? Did you see that governor turn the dogs onto those civil rights protesters?"

"Rome wasn't built in a day, Miss Orphanides. When you get a little older and I hope a lot wiser, you'll understand that progress happens slowly. But now, onto Gettysburg . . ."

"I just don't know how we can study the Civil War without also looking at the daily newspapers."

"I'm sorry if the restraints of the curriculum don't agree with you, Miss Orphanides. All I know is that we have to get to the Industrial Revolution by the end of May and I'm one week behind. Now, may I?"

Agafya put her legs out in the now familiar posture, passive, yet clearly defiant. Mr. White went to Gettysburg. Agafya stared out the window.

One day when Brian was walking home he noticed Agafya on the boulevard. "Hey, I didn't know you lived down here," Brian said.

"You never asked," she said, smiling. "I live two blocks from you."

"How do you know where I live?"

"Because I'm curious."

"About me?"

"Don't flatter yourself, about everyone and everything."

"You don't seem to fit too well in class, if I can say that."

"You're as perceptive as a piece of cake, if I may say that."

"I'm sorry, I just . . ."

"Don't worry, of course I don't fit in. How could I, I was born on Mars."

"What?"

"Just kidding, Miller."

"You called me Miller."

"Don't your friends?"

"Yea, but . . ."

"I'm not your friend?"

"Well I guess."

Brian realized that she had his head spinning and he easily could imagine what she was doing to Mr. White. Brian even felt himself feeling sorry for him.

"You want to come up and see where I live?"

"Well I . . ."

"I'm not twisting your arm."

"OK . . . I have some time."

"Don't do me any big favors. I was just asking."

"No, I'd like to."

They walked along quietly.

"Here it is," Agafya said.

It was another nondescript six-floor brick apartment building just like the one Brian lived in. They took the elevator up to the third floor, got out, and Agafya opened her door.

Once inside, Brian had an inkling about where Agafya "came from." It was an apartment different from any others he had ever seen. Most of the apartments Brian was familiar with had fake antique chairs or Scandinavian modern's simple lines. This place was decorated in clutter, the type of clutter he couldn't imagine adults living in.

There were books everywhere like autumn leaves on the ground. There were paintings, real paintings on every surface of the walls; paintings that really looked like something and others that were just as messy as the apartment. There was a piano, a big piano in the hall. There was a hammock in the living room and there were colorful clothes everywhere, like the ponchos she wore.

"Here, leave your books and we'll go into my room. You want some apple cider?"

"You mean juice?"

"No, cider. We drive upstate to get some each fall, freeze it, and thaw it out for the time of year when there is none for sale."

"OK, I'll have some."

Agafya got two glasses of the dark, muddy-looking cider and took it into her room.

"Follow me," she said.

In her bedroom, there were also paintings everywhere, a guitar next to her bed, record albums, and candles. Brian had never seen candles except on birthday cakes.

"Here, I'll put a record on. You like jazz?"

"I don't really know."

"Here. Check this out, Miles Davis. The greatest trumpet player in the world!"

Some soft trumpet music came on and Agafya started to sing to it.

"So you think I don't fit in?"

"Well, not really . . ."

"Don't start getting all polite with me. I don't believe in politeness. It's like a perfect façade covering a termite-eaten house. It's phony."

"OK . . . Yes, I don't think you really fit in. You're kind of . . . different."

"You're right, of course. I've never fit in. I ask too many questions."

"How come?"

"Because no one else does. Maybe if someone asked questions I wouldn't have to."

"Why do you feel that people have to ask questions?"

"Because who is Mr. White anyway? He's just a teacher. He doesn't know everything."

"He's pretty smart."

"So are a lot of people. The smartest admit they don't know everything."

Agafya was always saying and thinking things that seemed either light-years ahead or behind Brian and he couldn't figure out which. He never could figure out how to even continue a conversation with her. Her words just stopped him in his tracks. Sometimes he felt that she was talking from another, more intelligent world, one that in his simple, normal way, he couldn't comprehend . . . though, he had to admit, one he was quite fascinated by.

"Listen," Agafya said, as she picked up a guitar. "I'm working on a song." She began to strum the guitar and started to sing some sort of song he had never heard. It wasn't like the jazz but some sort of earnest-sounding story about a woman and a man in love that ends tragically.

"Folk music," she said.

Brian looked around her room and there were albums and books everywhere. Bill Evans piano music, John Coltrane, Miles Davis, Pete Seeger, Joan Baez, and a skinny kid. She put on his record and as he began, Brian couldn't stop laughing.

"You got to be kidding. What kind of voice is that? The neighborhood cat can sing better!"

"Bob Dylan. His first album. He's great, huh?"

And books, books everywhere, like plants on the side of the road in the summer.

Suddenly there was a knock at her door.

"May I come in?"

There was a woman in blue jeans, the same age as Brian's mother, who was wearing a blue men's-style shirt and had bright blue eyes.

"This is my mother. Mom, this is Brian. He lives down the road."

"Hello Brian," the woman said.

Soon there was someone else in at the door: a man with graying hair and a little beard on his chin.

"Well," he said, "who do we have here?"

"Dad, my friend, Brian. Brian, my dad."

"Nice to meet you," said the man.

I wondered what he was doing home, and almost like she could read my mind Agafya said, "My dad is a writer; he works from home. My mom teaches piano."

"They work from home? I've never heard about anyone doing that."

"Yea, they didn't want to take the crowded subway, so when they got out of art school, they tried to figure out a way they could work without commuting."

"Cool," Brian said, really meaning it.

Brian realized it was getting to be time to go to dinner and said goodbye. Agafya thanked him for coming over. Her mother and father were at the door.

"Hey, come again," said her father.

"Nice to meet you," her mother said.

They both seemed to be much less formal than his parents or the parents of his friends.

Walking back home, Brian realized what a different world he had just come from. As he came into his room, with still traces of his youth . . . baseball team pennants, gloves, flags from their trips, he realized again how different their worlds were and kind of sensed that it would be a long time before they would match . . . if ever.

The next day in school Mr. White announced the beginning of what was for him the happiest month in the school year . . . Science Fair Month! Science fairs happened in every school in New York City since the 1950s when our country worried that we were "falling behind" the scientific achievements of the Soviet Union. So, every year, every school, in their cafeterias, gyms, multipurpose rooms would stage a science fair, the winners of which would go to the the district and then to the city, state, and finally, if they continued to win, to the nationals.

"Boys and girls," started Mr. White, "as you know this is science fair time. Science has been responsible for our great successes as a people and as a nation . . ."

"Also our greatest horrors!"

Oh, oh, there she went!

"What is that Miss Orphanides, who still, after all this time, clearly does not understand the etiquette of hand raising?"

"I said that science has also been responsible for some of the worst disasters of our history as well."

"I suppose you don't use the electric lightbulb, Miss Orphanides?"

"That's not what I referring to, Mr. White. I was referring to Hiroshima and to the atomic bomb."

"Yes, war is terrible, but unfortunately, a necessity."

"It wasn't necessary to create or drop the bomb, Mr. White, and now we have more nuclear bombs than we need. We could blow the world up 100 times."

"Very interesting, Miss Orphanides. I suppose that you would have liked to be under the control of the Germans, or the Japanese now. How is your Japanese by the way, Miss Orphanides?"

"By the time we dropped the bomb, the Germans were officially defeated and the Japanese were well on their way."

"That's a very nice theory, Miss Orphanides, and when you finally get your head out of the sand, come talk with me. Now, back to science."

Again, Agafya assumed the "contrarian" position. Legs and now boots outstretched, head back.

"So, boys and girls, I'd like you to begin choosing a project for the science fair and if you'd like, choose a partner, and by next Monday, please be ready to tell us."

The science fair was a *big* deal. Not for Brian, though. He had the skill of a three-year-old when it came to science, or for putting *anything* together for that matter. He'd get model airplanes and they'd end up on the floor of his bedroom in more pieces than there were when he removed it from the package. His last year's project with his partner, Ernie DePietro, was trying to discover if a thick straw would sip soda faster than a thin one. It was his way of getting to drink soda in school.

Or the year before, that now quite famous project, "What will grow better, a plant put outside at night or in the day?" Poor asparagus fern! But for most everyone in school, the science fair was greeted with a combination of excitement, reverence, and nervousness. As the day of its beginning arrived, the dealing began as kids figured out how to team up with the smartest boys and girls. Those kids, who before Science Fair Month, were pretty low on the popularity scale, suddenly became the most popular kids in school. It was as if they were suddenly star quarterbacks being recruited for some college football team.

Brian noticed the maneuvering as early as lunch that day. Henry Scholl offered Freddy Rodman some Twinkies and began talking about going to a movie together. Jeff Rosen sat next to Vladimir Kasselbaum, who had just moved from Russia and talked very little English, but was reputed to be a science genius. And Susan Fisher, queen bee of the girls, promised to invite Florence Haddix to her next party if she would just be her partner for the science fair. Yes, the science fair made some strange bedfellows, with the nerdy and the cool finally lying down together, like the lions and lambs in the

Bible. Of course the harmony would last as long as the last science exhibit needed to be built.

Brian was trying to figure out what he needed to do and with whom. He knew that the exploding volcano idea would be taken soon enough and if he didn't hurry, all the smart, nerdy kids would be taken and he would be left with someone equally bad in science or worse . . . like Richard Wallerstein, who was walking toward him.

"Hi Brian. I have this great idea for a project that maybe we can do together. We could see how long it takes a piece of bread to grow mold?"

"I don't think so."

"How about the old 'tooth in the Coke' trick?"

"No"

"How about . . ."

Brian stopped him right there. He didn't really like Richard. He spit when he talked and was no better than he was in either coming up with projects, or executing them.

When Brian returned home, he called Ronnie to see what he was going to do for the fair. He was working with the science genius, Ali Marcotte. Ali's father was a physicist and although he had no idea what he was going to do, he was sure that Ali's dad would help them out. Felix Rosenstein was going to see what substances he could use to build a tower up to the ceiling of the cafeteria, testing everything from cotton to bubble gum. Steve Rosenberg, whose father owned a movie theater, was going to ask his father if the temperature in the theater had any effect on customers' enjoyment of the film. Walking to school the next day, Brian still hadn't picked a project and today was the day all kids had to choose!

It seemed as though everyone had a project—Howard Groopman's "Will a three-legged ant walk only 3/4 the speed as one with all four legs?" . . . Chrissy Conrad's "At what temperature will a Barbie doll's arm melt?" . . . Leanne Jefferson's "How long will it take different foods to smell bad?" . . . and now, finally Brian's turn! His head spun . . .

"Uh . . . How to make a baseball."

There, he said it and was committed to it. He had no idea how he would study it, but at least he had a topic.

And finally . . . "OK, Miss Orphanides," said Mr. White. "What are you going to do for the science fair?"

Agafya took her legs down from her usual position, sat up straight in her chair, and looked Mr. White right in the eye and said, "I'm making the world stop." The class didn't know how to react. Some sat stunned, some laughed. Bryan just sat there thinking about how nuts this girl really was.

Mr. White just couldn't be bothered. All he said was, "Miss Orphanides, please just make sure that you let us know when."

The last month of school was devoted completely to discussing science and building science fair projects. In the morning they studied the history of science, everything from the use of leeches for healing to a debate about whether or not we could ever travel faster than the speed of light. In the afternoon, they built their projects.

Brian looked up "baseballs" in the encyclopedia and wrote to Spaulding, the baseball manufacturer. He even opened one up and had the string from the ball unraveling over the floor of the classroom. Leanne's cheese was beginning to stink. And Barbie Doll arms were turning up looking like they had been though a war. Agafya just sat with her eyes closed. Mr. White was so excited about her silence that he didn't even say a word.

Every day the kids came in and excitedly told about their discoveries during the night and then in a blink of an eye, they were a day away from the fair. Nervous energy permeated the classroom. They were even told that the superintendent of their district would be coming to the fair. They were proud. Only Agafya seemed unaffected. On the way home from school, Brian saw her.

"Hey!"

"Hey," she said.

"It's cool that the superintendent is coming to our school, huh?"

"Not really. He's just a guy."

Brian had trouble arguing with that.

"Brian, I'm really concerned with this war in Vietnam. The French got out and now we are taking over. I really don't think we belong there, do you?"

"Uhmmm . . ."

Brian really wanted to say something. He really did. But he didn't even know where Vietnam was. He felt that he should know and felt that Agafya expected him to know and that it was a compliment that she asked for his opinion, but all he could think about was his science fair project and whether or not the Yankees would win tonight's game.

Brian asked Agafya how she was doing with her science project.

"Still working on it. It's not easy to stop the world, you know."

"I suppose."

How else was he supposed to respond to that?

Finally, the day of the science fair arrived. Kids came to school by car, having been driven by parents who helped unload their projects and bring them down into the basement, where each class was given a designated area. There were small volcanoes, bottles of undefined liquids, models of dinosaurs, and even a real caged animal or two. Bryan came in and put down his unraveled baseball on a desk with the ubiquitous oak tag diagram in the back. He went upstairs to his class.

"Well, students," said Mr. White. "Today is our big day." His tie was extra tightly tied and his shirt as crisp as a fresh head of iceberg lettuce. "I've been looking at some of your projects and may I say, they are quite wonderful. You must have done a lot of work on them. I can tell." Suddenly, the chimes went off on the intercom. Mr. Tauchner came on.

"Boys and girls, we are all very proud of you today. Your projects show how much we, in PS 196, care about science and the future of our beloved country. Teachers, can we have the sixth grade come down first and stand by their projects and would the other grades come down according to your schedule to begin your science fair tour? Again, wonderful job, boys and girls!"

So, everyone went down the stairs to the cafeteria where wheels turned, dogs barked, volcanoes smoked, music blared, teeth rotted, frogs swam. Those who had to stay with their exhibits to demonstrate how they worked, did. Those whose exhibits were "self-explanatory" walked around. Brian walked with two of his buddies, Burton and David. There were the usual . . . solar systems, hand creams, worms and ant houses, and a few he hadn't seen before . . . the roller coaster ride with a fish in a bowl and the hamster that was strapped onto an electric train crashing into a brick over and over again.

Suddenly a stir went through the room. Brian and his friends looked away from the rat generating electricity and in came Mr. Tauchner with Mr. Brunetti, the district superintendent. Mr. Tauchner seemed so proud and yet so small compared to Mr. Brunetti. It was the first time, Brian realized, that their principal took a backseat to anyone. Even when he talked to parents he had a kind of superior attitude, like he was someone famous. But now, for the first time, it was he who wanted to please.

Mr. Tauchner took Mr. Brunetti by the arm and went with him from project to project . . . well, sort of. He skipped Brian's baseball, Howard's project with the three-legged ants, and a few others, but went straight to the smart kids' projects; Andy's estimation of the time it would take to go to the various planets, Kenneth's models of undersea cities, and Sheryl's beehive. Unpredictably, he walked over to Agafya's "exhibit." She said exhibit, but Brian wasn't sure one could call it that. Agafya was sitting on a colored carpet, cross-legged, with a candle burning in front of her.

Mr. White noticed where the two were heading and tried to head them off and direct them to another project, but Mr. Brunetti seemed to be intrigued by the girl with the crossed legs. All the kids sensed a very interesting confrontation, so everyone gathered around as Mr. White cringed and as Mr. Tauchner tried to keep up his best "We are so proud" façade.

Mr. Brunetti asked, "So young lady. What is your project about?"

"I am trying to stop life on earth for a second. We have been moving faster and faster and I want to see if by slowing myself down, I might be able to give everything a rest."

Mr. Brunetti acted like he had mistakenly tried to have a real conversation with someone mentally deranged. Mr. Tauchner laughed and Mr. White turned red. Agafya closed her eyes again and chanted something like "Om . . . Om . . . Om." Those who had gathered around the exhibit began to laugh and in spite of trying to hold it in, the laughter kept coming. Mr. Tauchner and Mr. Brunetti started to walk away when suddenly . . . the lights went out. Out! Everything that was powered by electricity . . . the trains . . . the roller coaster . . . the refrigerator for milk, just stopped! Everyone stood there in silence and darkness, for one short minute, until as suddenly as it went off, the electricity came back on and all was again busy, loud, and normal.

Agafya opened her eyes and smiled.

Mr. Tauchner and Mr. Brunetti laughed nervously. Mr. White just stood there.

Ernie DePietro spoke first.

"Mr. White, why did that happen?"

The eyes of the class turned to Mr. White, waiting to hear some sort of explanation for the blackout. Agafya looked at him and he at her. Mr. White stood there silently for what felt like forever until he said,

"I don't know."

The science fair ended. The underwater colony took first place and went to the district fair, where it got honorable mention. The three-legged ants took second and got nothing in the district and Brian's project ended up, once again, in the garbage.

Agafya changed after that day. She was less rebellious and more involved. She and Mr. White didn't argue so much as discuss ideas about science, philosophy, and even the Vietnam War, a war Agafya was continually trying to call everyone's attention to with an ever-increasing number of buttons on her book bag. On the last day of school Brian walked Agafya home. By now they were kind of friends. "So," Brian said, "your first year in Forest Hills is over. How did you like it?"

"It was OK, I guess. No harm."

"You going to Halsey Jr. High with us next year?"

"Nah, my mom and dad bought a VW bus and we are going to take a trip around the US. I'll be homeschooled, I guess."

"Cool."

"I guess. But next year I want to come back and see how all you jerks are doing. I'm hoping that while I'm away, you'll be organizing the opposition to the war."

Brian knew he had to ask her one thing.

"Agafya, how come after that science fair, you and Mr. White started to get along?"

She looked up at me and smiled.

"One time, just once, I just wanted to hear him say, 'I don't know.'"

QUESTIONS FOR STUDENTS

- Have you ever been the new kid in school and if so, what was it like?
- How did they act and why do you think they acted in that way? Have you ever noticed how the new kids behaved one way when they first got to school and another after they settled in?
- How would you have liked to have been treated on your first days in a new school? How have you treated others?
- If you've ever been the new kid in school, did you think your teacher treated you OK during your adjustment period? If so, how did he or she treat you and if not, how could they have done better?
- Has there ever been a kid in your class who just seemed "different" from everyone else? If so, how did you and your friends react to them? Did you come to respect their differences or were you always "put off" by them?
- Do you think they could have acted differently to "fit in"? Do you think that was their responsibility and if so, why, and if not, why not?

THOUGHTS FOR STUDENTS

This story of Agafya is a story about a new kid in school, one who seems to be just a little smarter than everyone else and her intelligence set her apart from her new class. She was nonetheless interesting to the class, and they were torn about whether to "take her in" or to isolate her. She made most of the kids both curious and scared. It was as if she were from another planet.

She seemed weird and yet, in a strange way, seemed to understand what was really going on in school better than anyone did. Her family was different from the family of all the other kids. Her interests were different from her classmates and the way she treated people in authority was different from how everyone else did. Yet, like all of them, when it came down to it, she just wanted to be recognized for who she was and for the talents and intelligence she possessed.

It is difficult being the new kid in school. You look around and everyone is different from kids in your old school. You try to figure out what people are wearing, how they are acting, what words and accents they use, who is cool and who isn't. It is like you don't know how to swim and someone throws you into the deep end of the pool. Since most of us have been or will be the new kid in school, it is up to us to figure out how to make that experience better for that new kid and of course for you, if you happen one day, to be the kid who's new. Sometimes with a new kid there is a tendency to "lock down," to gather up your friends and to not let any new person through the gates of your community.

Sometimes, the new person, if they seem interesting, athletic, pretty/handsome, or smart, is taken in right away. If they don't watch out and/or if they read the "cues" wrong . . . like starting to flirt with someone else's boy- or girlfriend, the initial openness quickly becomes rejection. It is really difficult to be the new kid in school. You want to impress everyone, yet you don't want to seem like a braggart. You want to be liked, but you worry about choosing the "wrong" people to be friends with.

New kids in school sometimes act very strangely. They try to pick fights to show how strong they are. They sometimes brag about things that are often exaggerated because they want to impress others. Sometimes new kids go out of their way to get on their teacher's nerves in an effort to "show off." It is probably good not to judge anyone too harshly after a week or two. After all, you wouldn't want to be judged by such a superficial sampling.

Helping a new kid adjust is truly an act of kindness and compassion and one you certainly would appreciate if the shoe were on the other foot. If you can, help him or her out by asking if they need any help finding things or by inviting them to sit with you at lunch or to hang out with you and your friends during recess. Trying to help someone out when they first arrive at your school doesn't mean you have to be committed to them forever. It just means that you understand how difficult it is to be "new" and you want to help make their adjustment to a new environment as smooth as you can.

Remember, by reaching out to a new person it not only makes them feel better, but it will make you feel better and bigger. By helping others, you extend yourself and also create opportunities for yourself to learn and maybe, to make a new friend.

THOUGHTS FOR TEACHERS

Curriculum and Pedagogical Suggestions: English and Geography

- What are your responsibilities as a teacher to make sure that the "new kid" gets an opportunity to "land" smoothly?
- How can the other students learn something from their arrival?
- How can you make the new child's transition smooth while watching for signs that it isn't?

This is certainly easier in an elementary school classroom where your students are with you for most of the day. It is much easier to monitor how a "new kid" is doing. You can see it in their face, in the way they carry themselves, and notice if they are befriended by anyone. You also have more time to initiate conversation in your classroom about what it is like being a "new kid."

In a middle school while a kind of "soft landing" is often needed more, it is unfortunately more difficult to accomplish. However, there are things you can do to help the middle school students feel more comfortable during their arrival/adjustment period. For one, a simple greeting and a few questions to the new student would model respectful curiosity. As you certainly already know, don't make the "new kid" feel like they are being cross-examined. Nonetheless, a few questions and a short welcome will help make a student more comfortable and will also give other students a way to approach him or her.

Next, in English the role of a "new kid" as well as the class's behavior toward them is certainly material for writing. Use it for fiction and personal memoir. Writing from the perspective of being a "new kid" and from the point of view of the existing class can be used as prompts for writing.

In social studies you can devote some time to where the new student came from in order to acquaint students with other parts of the nation/world and again, to provide some gist for conversation that would show off some of the new student's expertise. You can also use the opportunity of having a new student to study and to discuss the immigrant experience in our country. What was it like and still like for any of your students or their relatives or neighbors to first arrive in the United States? How does an immigrant maintain elements of their former selves while creating new behaviors, forms of language, psychological expectations as they work at becoming "American"?

Remember, a "new kid" is like anyone else, except they are new. Accepting and understanding the thoughts and feelings of a new kid teaches empathy and compassion, and making that new kid feel OK is an act of kindness. New kids make poor choices, cultural faux pas, and so forth, but don't we all?

Chapter Seven

Two Stubborn College Kids
(Based on an Appalachian Folktale)

Two college boys shared a room in an apartment near school and were the best of friends. Their names were Artie and Carlos. Artie was tall and skinny and looked like a scarecrow. He had long sandy hair that swept back into a ponytail. He always wore flannel shirts and jeans ripped at the knees. He wore boots that were never tied, with laces that flopped around as if they didn't know what to do next. He had the beginnings of a blond beard and mustache that pushed up past the skin on his face like the first growth of plants in the spring.

Artie liked to listen to alternative rock and folk, the bands Phish and Further, and he loved, *loved* Kurt Cobain and Nirvana, especially the *MTV Unplugged* Kurt Cobain. In college, he studied forestry because he wanted to sit in the woods, write poetry, and play his songs on his beloved Les Paul guitar that his uncle bought for him and that he *always* kept next to his bed. He grew up in Portland, Oregon, loved to hike, and was into white-water rafting and extreme snowboarding.

Carlos was originally from San Pedro de Macoris, in the Dominican Republic, where many great baseball shortstops come from, but his family moved to Providence, Rhode Island, when he was three years old. However, he went back to the Dominican Republic every summer to see friends and relatives. Carlos was pretty short, with eyes as dark as a starless night, and hair that was cropped close to his head, like a lawn in the suburbs. He had a thin line of a beard and always wore a black beret and a cross around his neck. He was a rapper and created beats with his computer. Sometimes at dorm parties he'd DJ using some of his own creations that many seemed to like. He also had a number of drums and especially liked to jam with Artie on the guitar and he, the Djembe.

Even though Artie and Carlos came from different worlds, they started to quickly hang out when they found each other their first year of college and decided that the next year they would be roommates. It worked out great. They walked to school with their iPods, Artie listening to the Pixies and the Ramones and Carlos to Latin rap and reggaeton. On the way to class they'd sometimes even switch iPods and Carlos began to really like Rage Against the Machine and Firefox while Artie got a taste for merengue.

At night they would alternate cooking dinner. They learned to like what each other cooked. Artie had learned vegetarian cooking from his mom and dad, who he liked to say were "old hippies." He cooked great casseroles with tofu, which Carlos never thought he'd like as much as he did. And Carlos often cooked his grandmother's fried chicken and plantains that Artie learned to cook for a late-night snack. Their apartment was kind of funky, but the boys kept it quite neat. They found a couch and a kitchen table at the thrift store, some chairs on the street. Carlos's parents brought up some old family dishes and Artie's parents sent them a blender, a small oven, and an espresso machine that they both loved.

The two boys really liked each other. Artie once visited Carlos's house for Christmas and Carlos hung out in Portland with Artie and his friends. Artie and Carlos were planning to go to the Dominican Republic together for spring break.

Oh sure, there were always things that annoyed the boys about each other. Carlos didn't like that Artie never washed the pans he cooked and with left them soaking on the countertop near the kitchen. Artie didn't like that Carlos's music was turned up too loud while he was studying. Carlos didn't like that Artie never cleaned the toilet. Artie didn't like that Carlos left his clothes in the living room. Just the regular annoyances people have when they live together. Nothing got between them, though, because they put their friendship before their disagreements. In fact, they never even mentioned what they didn't like about each other's habits. They just stuffed those things inside as if the things that bothered them about one another were sleeping bags stuffed into its bag.

One day Artie came home from a tough day at school. He had gotten a lower grade on a test than he thought he would, didn't get into a class he had requested for the following semester, and saw a girl he liked walking on campus with another guy. It was not a good day for Carlos either, who had been laid off from his part-time job cooking at a local diner and then had lost the key to his bicycle lock and had to smash the lock to get it open. Carlos was already sitting on the couch listening to some salsa when Artie walked in. For Artie, the sound of the loud music was just too much for his already filled head.

"Shut the music off!" Artie yelled.

Those were not the words that Carlos wanted to hear. He felt that he needed his loud Latin music to get him out of the mood he was in and he ignored Artie.

"I said, turn the music off!" Artie said and was again ignored by Carlos.

"Turn it off!"

When once more there was no reaction, Artie went into *his* room and turned his music, Foo Fighters, even louder, which drove Carlos crazy. So, he turned *his* music still louder and of course, Artie turned up the volume of *his* music and so on and so on until the sound of the dueling music was deafening!

Artie's eyes focused on Carlos's pants and shirts from the night before that had been left on the couch.

"Why don't you ever put your clothes away?" he shouted.

"Why don't you ever clean your pans?" Carlos shouted back.

"You are a real pig!" said Artie.

"Me? You are a spoiled brat who didn't know how to cook until I taught you and who doesn't *ever* clean the toilet!"

"You're the slob!"

"Yeah, right."

"I can't believe that I ever chose you to room with."

"You chose me? You chose me? Out of pity I agreed to live with you."

"You couldn't even find a dog to live with you!"

"I found you!"

Their words became more and more hurtful and instead of stopping to apologize, each boy began to feel more and more disrespected, making the matter worse. The boys sat on the couch in silence, that is, except for the loud music. Every once in a while they stared at each other and then to the apartment, noticing how messy and dirty it actually looked and of course blaming each other for what they saw.

Finally, Carlos spoke. "Whoever talks or gets up first, except to go to the bathroom, has to clean the apartment."

Artie agreed. "Deal."

Neither of the boys spoke, but the clashing music continued. Day after day this silence (except for the music) continued. The appointment got messier and messier and messier. The boys' dirty clothes sprawled over all of the furniture. Newspapers were piled everywhere. The kitchen and toilets were so dirty that even the boys could barely tolerate going into them . . . and the smell!

But did one of the boys lift a finger? Did either speak? What do you think?

One night, as the boys were falling asleep on the couch watching TV, the door to their apartment slowly opened. Into the apartment walked two men, whose faces were covered by scarves. They walked in and saw the boys and were going to leave until they realized that they were asleep. The two men looked around the mess for things to steal. One of the men saw the computer in Carlos's room and he began to carry it out when he tripped over a soda bottle on the floor . . . and the boys woke up.

They were both startled to see the thieves and were going to scream, when they both realized that if they did, they would lose their "competition" and have to clean the apartment. So they stayed silent and didn't move.

The thieves, realizing that the boys had awakened, were going to run, but then realized that neither of the boys were going to say or in fact do anything. So, they began helping themselves to whatever they could find . . . more computers, backpacks, hiking boots, sleeping bags, tents, the espresso machine, the toaster oven, the blender, CDs, and even the prized Les Paul guitar! They began treating the objects in the boys' apartment as if they were plates of food at a buffet breakfast! But as much as it pained the boys to see their prized possessions stolen, neither said a word, nor moved!

The thieves left the apartment just as the boys heard a car door slam and they knew it meant they would never, ever see their precious possessions again. They simultaneously got up, ran out of the apartment, and together yelled, "Thief!" unfortunately just in time to watch the car pull away.

As the boys walked silently back to and into their apartment they looked around and noticed that the only thing left was . . . garbage! Newspapers, soda bottles, food wrappers, and packaging of all kinds. Finally the boys were able to see the mess they were living in . . . and wouldn't you would think that finally they would have had enough of being stubborn? But . . .

"You spoke first."

"You did!"

"No way."

"Yes, way!"

"No way."

"Yes, way."

And the boys continued and to this day, continue. If you are near this college and you happen to notice an apartment with the garbage flowing out the windows and doors, walk in, if you can, that is, and you will see and hear those two stubborn boys, going at it, back and forth, as their apartment gets dirtier and dirtier each day.

"You spoke first."

"No, you spoke first."

"No, you did."

"No, you did."

QUESTIONS FOR STUDENTS

- Who was the most stubborn, Carlos or Artie? Why?
- What makes people stubborn?
- How might the boys have handled things better to preserve their friendship and their apartment?
- Have you ever been through a difficult moment with a friend? How did you deal with it if you did? How could you have dealt with it better?
- Could an apology have changed anything and if so how?

THOUGHTS FOR STUDENTS

This story is a version of an old folktale I heard a long time ago. In it, the two people involved were a husband and wife. They too allowed their stubbornness to get the better of them. To make a point about who was right and who was wrong, the boys in this story and the couple in the other lose everything they have, including in this instance, their friendship.

Whenever people are good friends there are times when their friendship will be tested. How we deal with those moments determines how and if the friendship will continue. In this case, as is often the case when friendship is tested, it was at a particularly stressful time for each boy individually. It makes sense, doesn't it? When we feel the most vulnerable, unhappy, and tense, we feel like we have less "space" for understanding and generosity. At these moments, unspoken resentments, annoyances, and anger can bubble up to the surface and explode.

This is a good reason why it is important to let people know about any difficulty you have toward them as soon as you can. It is not fair to hold bad feelings toward a friend without letting them know. When feelings remain hidden, you leave your friend no way to correct something they might want to change. When you finally do "blow up," they have no clue why you are so angry about what seems to be a little thing that might have been easy to take care of, had they known it bothered you.

In this story, both boys didn't like some things about one another, things that could have been easily fixed. For instance, Artie could have asked Carlos to turn his music down or Carlos could have asked Artie to wash the pans after he was done cooking. Had that happened, their anger toward each other would not have been permitted to fester and "boil over" with so much pent-up anger and resentment.

Once these little annoyances are permitted to sit with you, they are much more difficult to deal with. In this case, both boys got defensive when confronted and attacked the other. Once that happened the initial problem between the boys was hidden under fog and a whole new set of problems and resentments emerged. Neither got to talk about what was really bothering them that day. Had the issues between the two boys been spoken about earlier, rather than fighting with each other about the mutually held, small annoyances of daily life, they might have been able to help each other with the larger problems each was facing that day.

The quicker we address those things that bother us toward one another, the better it will be. Living with someone and/or being close friends with someone is never easy, but it is worth investing the time and having the courage to keep the lines of communication clean and the anger low.

We all know how much courage it takes a soldier, a firefighter, or a police officer to do their job well, but how many think of the courage it takes to tell a friend that they did something that hurt you or that made you angry. You put yourself out there and out of your comfort zones. Those who can enter into the often rough seas of friendship are "relationship warriors," heroically entering the difficult world of friendship, not without fear, but with courage as well!

THOUGHTS FOR TEACHERS

Curriculum and Pedagogical Suggestions: Mythology

You can use this story to engage your students in a study of the "hero." The hero traditionally has been someone who overcame fear to save the lives of one or more people. The warrior, the soldier, and so on all fall under this umbrella. Joseph Campbell in *A Hero of Ten Thousand Faces* looked at the idea of the hero and saw him or her as someone who is leading an ordinary life until they hear a call, or is chosen to leave their "comfort zone." He or she dedicates himself or herself to being present for the challenges that they are confronted with when they do. While there is never full mastery, the hero realizes that with every obstacle overcome, for every hurdle leaped, he or she becomes a stronger, deeper, and more empathetic person.

This alternative version of what makes a hero is important for boys and girls. Rather than the heroes that most boys and girls see and identify with—the soldier, the police officer, the sports athlete (all of course heroes in their own right)—this other kind of hero tackles the difficult and often incomprehensible world of relationships, be they platonic or intimate.

In this world, to be able to clearly articulate anger, feelings, and/or thoughts with another person is a heroic act. It puts us in strange and new territory, taking us out of our sense of control and familiarity and demands that we become a new person, able to tell another what about them is bothering us while not releasing ourselves from culpability.

The more we are able to enter this world with intentionality, clarity, and vulnerability, the better at it we will become and the more competent we will feel to navigate the world of emotions and self-knowledge. This confidence spills out into other areas of your and your students' lives and you grow in your ability to say what needs to be said and to recognize how honesty keeps the conversational and psychological channels of personal relationships unclogged.

Can your students become "relationship warriors"? Can you help transform their understanding that "heroes" not only inhabit the worlds of war and athletics, but can exist in the world of interpersonal relationships? Will students be able embrace this new vision of "the hero" and learn to do the personal work necessary to become more powerful and self-aware?

With effort and through modeling, you can convince them that it is within their best interests to become a "relationship warrior." After all, in life and in relationships you can be stuck in the mud and spin your wheels or you can get a piece of cardboard and stick it under the tires. Your students need to realize that they have the choice about whether or not to keep spinning their wheels when it comes to dealing with difficulties in a relationship or to leave that too-familiar place and see what else is on the drive.

Where in your curriculum can you introduce your students to these "relationship warriors"?

Many novels, films, and music directed toward middle school students are "relationship" oriented. Study those examples with your students and discuss choices made and paths taken and not taken in the various art forms.

Discuss the idea of "courage." In what arenas is it visible and discussed and where is it not? What does courage mean in relationships and how does one overcome fear in the interpersonal arena? Diplomacy is another area where relationships between people are very important and where lessons for your students in this area can be gleaned. Clarity of goals, finding common ground, and being willing to compromise can be the difference between war and peace. Devote time to studying efforts of and tactics for good diplomacy. At the same time, find examples where diplomacy failed, and study why.

Labor relations is yet another arena where interpersonal intelligence and courage are needed. How are two sides, whose goals seem often at variance with one another, able to come together on a mutually agreed upon settlement to a contentious conflict?

Remind your students that while conflict is everywhere, solutions are even more numerous. Many solutions boil down to this:

- Take responsibility for your actions
- Learn to apologize
- Understand and acknowledge the needs and points of view of the other person
- Come to an agreement about both parties' mutual responsibility for the conflict

- Find a mutually acceptable solution

Relationship warriors: If you don't think it takes courage, ask yourself how easy it was to tell someone you didn't want to be with them anymore, that you were angry with them for some reason, that you were hurt by them. Helping your students develop their "muscles" in this area will go a long way toward creating a sophisticated and brave community of students who are capable of navigating the shark-filled, scary waters of how people get along with each other with a commitment to honesty and directness.

Chapter Eight

The King and the Spider
Caught in Their Traps

In central India, a very long time ago, there was a particularly strong, power-ful, and if truth be told, blustering King. When he walked into a room, even the chairs shook with fear. This King lived in a big castle . . . a very, very big castle and he ate and slept at its top, in a room overlooking the desert. From there, he would sit, day after day, on his soft-as-a-cloud throne, watching for enemies that, well, he never really had. But there he sat, day after day, watching for his enemies, believing that someday there would be armies approaching. In reality, though, as I said, he had no enemies . . . NONE!

But when he considered that indeed, he might never have attackers, he thought,

"How can I be a King without enemies? A King must protect his people, or else why would a King be needed?"

So, he convinced himself, as well as his subjects, that there were in fact, enemies to fear and from his soft-as-a-cloud throne, every day he stood, or rather "sat" guard. If he saw so much as a sandstorm in the distance he imagined an army on horseback coming to attack. Being a thorough and organized King, he had a plan for those who would invade. He'd ring a giant bell and seven soldiers would position themselves at the seven stations above the covered ramp leading to the King's chambers. From there, the soldiers would prepare to drop seven weapons from seven holes cut from the covered ramp. Those seven soldiers were ready to drop: red-hot nails, boiling water, melting wax, heavy, heavy rocks, stinging spiders, poisonous snakes . . .

And . . .

Really, really sharp knives!

When on the rare occasion the King left his room above the rest of the castle, he would make sure the nails were red hot, the water boiling, the wax cooked and melted, the rocks heavy, the spiders angry, and that the knives were sharp enough to slice through a boulder like it was a slab of meat. No one would ever try to get past the guards at the castle's gate, because there really were no enemies. But the King still worried. "How do I remain a King if I don't have any enemies to protect my people from?" So, each time he saw even a little bit of sand, stirred up by a little bit of wind, he convinced himself that his enemies were coming and he rang the bell loudly and ordered his seven soldiers to get ready to drop the . . .

Red-hot nails, boiling water, melting wax, heavy, heavy rocks, stinging spiders, poisonous snakes . . .

And the . . .

Really, really sharp knives!

One morning, as the sun rose red over the eastern desert sky and the clouds looked like white fish swimming in a red and orange sea, an angry desert wind blew the sand. The King imagined that he was finally seeing the huge army of enemies that he always imagined he'd see, now readying to challenge the King for his rule.

The King ordered his seven horrible soldiers, from the seven horrible holes, to get ready to drop the . . .

Red-hot nails, boiling water, melting wax, heavy, heavy rocks, stinging spiders, poisonous snakes . . .

And . . .

Really, really sharp knives!

There really was no army moving toward the castle, however. NONE! But the King, even once he realized that the army he had feared was just blowing sand, was nonetheless *still* scared. "The soldiers are coming disguised as the wind," he yelled to his guards. And so, he forbade *anyone* from entering the castle, including even those who wanted to deliver food and water.

Soon, he began to worry that everyone in his castle, *but* his seven soldiers, might be part of the "invading army" and were indeed . . . spies! He ordered all the people who lived or worked in the castle to leave. "Out, spies! Out!" he yelled at those who shared the castle with him.

The only people left after the King's orders were the seven soldiers who were, as always, ready to drop from the seven holes, the . . .

Red-hot nails, boiling water, melting wax, heavy, heavy rocks, stinging spiders, poisonous snakes . . .

And . . .

Really , really sharp knives!

With food and water no longer delivered, the King and his seven soldiers were getting very, very thirsty and very, very hungry. The King ordered each of the seven soldiers, one at a time, to leave the castle and to return with food and drink. But none of the soldiers returned, each being afraid that the King

The King and the Spider Caught in Their Traps   79

would mistake them for an enemy and that their lives would be in danger and as they attempted entry. They worried that on their heads would drop . . .

Red-hot nails, boiling water, melting wax, heavy, heavy rocks, stinging spiders, poisonous snakes . . .

And . . .

Really, really sharp knives!

It wasn't long before each of the seven soldiers left the castle, never to return, leaving the King alone with his thoughts and weapons. The King worried that his trusted soldiers had joined the enemy army and were now plotting to take over the castle and his throne. To protect himself from this invasion, the King never stopped looking out the window, into the desert, looking for enemies, who, in fact, never did come.

Many, many years passed and still no one dared to walk back into that castle. Years had crumbled the castle's walls. Even then, though, after many years and the castle's crumbling walls, everyone nearby and from further away still remembered and were afraid of the seven holes with their seven horrible weapons. No one knew for sure whether or not the King still had soldiers ready to drop those dangerous weapons on the head of anyone who dared walk up the ramp to the room from where the King peered out into the desert.

It was many more years until finally, a local goat herder, in search of a stray, dared to walk through the crumbling castle gates and up the ramp, now filled with stones and sand fallen from the castle walls and roof and blown in from the desert. Above him he noticed the remnants of the seven holes, known then only in legend.

The goat herder walked carefully up the ramp, in awe of the castle's crumbling remains. The gold leaf paintings of great military victories that never actually occurred now were reduced to pictures of headless soldiers and legless camels. The once intricately decorated doors whose flowers and birds were once painted in turquoise now stood bare. The shops whose shelves were built with exotic woods found in the northern mountains and were once filled with fresh foods were now filled with flies and lizards.

The goat herder continued to walk, soon forgetting that he was even in search of his animal. Finally, at the top of the castle the goat herder came to the King's chambers. Opening its door that crumbled even as he thought of turning its handle, he looked in and noticed the King, or rather the King's skeleton, sitting on his soft-as-a-cloud throne with his head turned to the window, still looking out into the desert, for enemies that were never really there. Next to the King was a spider. Frightened by the goat herder's presence, the spider tried to flee, but he was unable to. The web that he had made caught him.

The goat herder returned to his village and of course told everyone what he had seen. To this day in central India you can hear this story that now serves to remind its listeners that the trap one sets for others could be the trap that catches you!

QUESTIONS FOR STUDENTS

- Why did the King believe he had to have enemies?
- Can you bring something about by worrying about it? Has that ever happened to you and if so when and what was it?
- Have you ever worried about something happening and you prepared and prepared for it and it never did occur?
- Have you ever noticed that people (or you) sometimes limit themselves by the behavior that had been previously used to protect themselves?
- Have you ever made life worse for yourself by behaving in a way you thought would help you?
- Do you think people worry too much and if so, why do you think they do so?

THOUGHTS FOR STUDENTS

Sometimes we behave in ways we used in the past, even after those behaviors are no longer useful to us. A behavior from the past, appropriate when originally used, when used in the present, can actually do us harm. For instance, in the Middle Ages, soldiers wore metal armor to protect themselves. The metal made it difficult to move but also was difficult to penetrate. Imagine that once the war was over and they returned home, they couldn't take off their armor. When they embraced their wives and children, instead of protecting them, it now kept them from being close to those they wanted to embrace.

War demands being on guard and suspicious. This behavior is useful when you are in constant danger from the known and unknown. However, when soldiers return home, they often find it difficult to adjust to civilian life. Their wariness often creates an emotional distance between themselves and their loved ones, often denying ex-soldiers the love and support they need to become part of "normal" life. They hold on to their wartime behavior long past its usefulness. Behavior that was appropriate and protective in one situation can become an roadblock to getting what you need in a new environment with new realities.

We all in our own way do that, don't we? The King certainly did, worrying and worrying and worrying about his imagined enemies and fulfilling the role he felt he needed to play in order to keep his power. Ultimately the very thing he worried about, his castle crumbling and his own death, happened because his fears created the world he feared. How many times have we behaved in ways that might have served us at one time, but as life went on, they were not only no longer necessary, but they also brought about what we feared?

For instance, let's imagine that when you were five years old and at the dinner table, you shared with your family that you had a crush on a girl in school and that she didn't share this crush. After sharing this intimate and painful detail of your life, your mom, dad, and older brother just laughed, telling you to "get over it" or maybe thought it was soooo "cute."

You felt they were minimizing the deep feelings you had. Not only might you not want to share any more intimate details about your life with them again, but you also might think that it is not safe to share those parts of your life with anyone. As you get older and people want to know who you are, you still don't share any personal information, still afraid to do so because of your past experience with sharing. Instead of getting the emotional support that everyone needs, you feel isolated and fearful.

So, while it might have been an intelligent decision to originally understand that your family was not a "safe" place for sharing intimate details of your life, imagining as you got older that the whole world was like that was not only incorrect, but also produced a reality that left you once again feeling alone.

Behavior that might have been at one time useful often becomes habitual. It happens without us even being aware. Angry responses to imagined threats, unwillingness to discuss a problem because conversations about things that concerned you often ended up in arguments, lying instead of telling the truth because "truth" was never celebrated, ignoring difficult decisions because each decision you made always seemed wrong. . . . These are all learned behaviors that again, while justifiable at one point in your life, can become unconscious and habitual, hurting you and those you care about.

Like the spider that was caught in its own web, we often get caught in our own past. We need to be aware of how we are reacting and behaving and realize that the present is not the past. When we behave from fear born from the past we often bring about what we fear.

Try to pay attention to how you react to life. Does your behavior get you what you want or doesn't it? Can you trace your behavior to a past pain and if so, is your behavior still appropriate? Can you change your behavior once you realize that it is rooted in a previous reality and no longer based on anything "real"? These are questions you need to ask yourself as you get older and as you create your own "story" rather than having the story written for you by the person you were.

THOUGHTS FOR TEACHERS

Curriculum and Pedagogical Suggestions: Diplomacy and Military History, History of Antiwar Movements

While the above story is quite psychological, it has its corollaries in the world of diplomacy and foreign policy. The Cold War was an example of fear-driven behavior creating fear-driven behavior. Innocent countries were caught in the cross fire and many people died in the process. The Cold War deprived both the Soviet Union and the United States of funding to modernize their infrastructure, to create meaningful work, and to provide for those who couldn't do so on their own. It also led to the needless loss of life of both countries' soldiers who were participants in wars in smaller countries serving as surrogates for the Cold War combatants.

Another example of poor choices motivated by fear was the reparations agreement following World War I when the Allies, fearful of a German military resurgence, gutted the German economy, creating resentment in the German population. This anger became political fodder for just the kind of German militarism that the Allies feared.

A third, was when the then president Bush's insisted that Iraq had "weapons of mass destruction." Whether he or his advisers believed that assertion is not fully known, but for a country still reeling from the World Trade Center bombings, this story became the justification for a war that is continuing to this day leading to much death and destruction, and to the destabilization of an entire region. In each of these cases fear and the actions generated as a result of it created the very situations that were feared.

While this subject is a bit more nuanced than many in this book and perhaps more difficult to get across, it is essential to cover. For students to change their behavior, they have to be aware not only of their behavior, but its derivation and its utility or not for present circumstances. Everyone has "vestigial behaviors," ones that were perhaps useful at one time, but are no longer. Helping your students understand that there is often a disconnect between their "vestigial behavior" and the results they desire in the present will help them to question how they act and why.

To make this point to your students you can use the example of soldiers returning from battle. As you know, many of these stories are filled with examples of inappropriate "vestigial behavior." In war, it is important for soldiers to be hypervigilant, but hypervigilance easily morphs into paranoia once a soldier returns to safer ground. When what the soldier needs upon returning home is vulnerability that permits others "in," the hypervigilance of war becomes instead an impediment to getting what a returning soldier really needs in his or her new circumstances.

Unfortunately, as teachers teach students about the importance of non-violent responses to provocation, they are faced with a disconnect between what they are trying to teach and violence-based and "retaliatory" actions taken by their own and other countries. Often this behavior can also be seen as "vestigial." These "retaliatory" actions can be interpreted as "reality" or hypocrisy depending upon one's point of view.

There are those, though, who have argued and indeed protested for non-violent alternatives to confrontations. However, while we ask our students to find alternatives to fighting, how often do schools teach about the history of resistance to war? There have been antiwar movements throughout the nineteenth century, from the Spanish–American War forward. Those arguing against World War I were imprisoned under the 1917 Alien and Sedition Act. The "ban the bomb" demonstrators of the 1950s were ridiculed. The United States government conducted surveillance against and launched tear gas at protestors in Washington, DC, during the Vietnam War.

Luckily though, there are many examples in government and beyond of people and organizations that have advocated for nonviolent solutions to potentially dangerous confrontations. For instance, former Congressman Kucinich, while in office, called for a Department of Peace that would work toward mediating conflicts and lessen the likelihood of war. There are many, many institutes for nonviolence and of course many, many examples where nonviolent resistance and mediation created the desired outcome of limiting violence that could have been part of a potential conflict.

One needs only to study the civil rights movement of the 1960s to see how a strategy based on taking the "higher road" changed the course of history, albeit of course, incompletely. Students need role models for behavior that avoids the unending dance of paranoia, violence, and retribution and the mistaken belief that the past should dictate the present.

Being able to look at one's behavior freshly and critically is an important corrective to a preservative pattern of recrimination and violence. Both the spider and the King didn't figure it out in time. Hopefully your students can.

Chapter Nine

The World's Fair and How Diana Learned That the World Wasn't Fair

The 1964–1965 World's Fair took place four miles from where Diana lived in New York City. Its theme was "Man in a Shrinking Globe in an Expanding Universe." The Fair took place at a time when space exploration and an increasingly sophisticated media were beginning to be part of everyday life, making the world seem smaller and the universe available for us to explore.

Diana took a special interest in the World's Fair from the first time she heard it was going to be practically her neighbor. Nowadays, it might seem strange to get so excited about a World's Fair, since the days of their importance has long gone by. At one time, though, they were big things, held all over the world in important cities wanting to make a statement about how important they were. The Eiffel Tower was built for the 1889 World's Fair in Paris, France, and the Space Needle for the 1962 Seattle World's Fair. The Fair's main attractions, however, were pavilions and rides created by participating nations and corporations.

The site for the World's Fair in Queens, the New York City borough Diana called home, was on a site called Flushing Meadows Park in Queens, where the New York Mets now play and where the US Open Tennis Center is located. Diana played Little League baseball there occasionally in the part of the park nearest to her home and often saw the Fair going up on her way home from Manhattan or to and back from LaGuardia Airport.

As soon as Diana heard about the New York City World's Fair coming to Queens, she began cutting out every article in the newspaper about its construction, new countries that were setting up pavilions, and famous people who would be coming to the opening, and putting them into a special World's Fair scrapbook she created. Most of the countries were from South America and Asia, with a few coming from Europe. When a new country or corporation announced it was building an exhibit at the Fair, the next thing Diana did was to tell Sam, who gave him all the vital statistics and history of that country or corporation.

Sam was an African American man who was one the smartest men Diana knew *and* he could hit a stickball into orbit. He delivered groceries from the grocery store on his thick red bicycle. Sam was about fifty. What Diana could never figure out was why he was doing a job done by teenagers earning money for dates when he was so smart.

"Any new countries announced?" Sam would say to Diana as he drove his bike full of groceries his way to a delivery.

"Yeah, Brazil," Diana said.

"Brazil," said Sam, "is the world's fifth largest country in area and by population. It is the only Portuguese-speaking country in the Americas and has a coastline of 4,655 miles. It borders every other South American country except Ecuador and Chile. Brazil was a colony of Portugal until it got its independence in 1822. In 1960, Brazil started to build a new capital city, Brasilia, in a place where there was nothing much before."

Sam's knowledge didn't stop at countries. He knew every US president and their wives, every state capital, the scientists who created important vaccines, inventions, and he spoke some Spanish, German, and French. He had even fought in World War II and knew every major battle of that war . . . oh, and he knew every stadium in the big leagues.

"Got to go," he said, "the meter's running!" And with that Sam would continue his ride to the next delivery.

In addition to keeping up with the World Fair articles, Diana also read a few of the headlines, those about the Cuban Missile Crisis, John Glenn orbiting the earth, Marilyn Monroe dying, the assassination of President Kennedy, and articles about the 1963 Civil Rights March in Washington where Martin Luther King Jr. made that famous "I have a dream" speech.

The civil rights movement in the southern part of the United States was really gaining steam around this time and you couldn't miss stories about it in the newspaper and on TV: James Meredith becoming the first Black student to enroll at the University of Mississippi and the violence and riots that sprang from it and that provoked President Kennedy to send in 5,000 federal troops in that state, the civil rights protests in Birmingham, Alabama, where the commissioner of public safety, Eugene "Bull" Connor, used fire hoses and police dogs on Black demonstrators and the articles about thirty-seven-year-old civil rights leader Medgar Evers, murdered outside his home. These stories were always in the newspapers and on TV back then.

Diana couldn't believe that there was even such a thing as segregation. It didn't make any sense that one group of people should be considered "inferior" and unworthy of even using the same water fountains and bathrooms as those used by others. Diana went to a very integrated YWCA sleepaway camp for many years and the thought that her friends and counselors who were African American were viewed as "less than" just because they were African American seemed so terrible and weird . . . if it were not so tragic, it would have been laughable.

The South seemed so "backward" and barbarous. The images of water cannons and police dogs attacking demonstrators filled the TVs on the evening news and the anger and hate coming from the faces of those who opposed the changes to the South's system of legalized racial segregation burned into her brain.

However, even as the civil rights demonstrations continued through the South, it was soon clear that the North would also become a site for this kind of agitation with protesters asking for fully integrated schools and equal opportunities for jobs. A group called CORE or the Congress of Racial Equality was leading the way. They, especially a CORE group from Brooklyn, NY, were using nonviolent yet disruptive tactics on bridges and public gathering places to make the point that the North, while superficially a better place for African Americans than the South, was, for those African Americans, not without its problems. While she was very sympathetic to civil rights efforts in the South, the idea that where she lived had racial problems just didn't ring true.

The demonstrations in the North really came home to him when the Brooklyn chapter of CORE announced that it was going to disrupt the opening day of the World's Fair with a "stall-in" on Grand Central Parkway, the main road leading into the Fair. The plan was to have 2,500 cars run out of gas on the way into the Fair, leaving thousands of fairgoers stuck.

Another demonstration was planned for inside the Fair's April 22 opening day, a demonstration called by an opponent of the Brooklyn group, a man named James Farmer, a national leader of CORE. He planned his demonstration for inside the Fair, planning for it to be peaceful. In spite of these differences, the demands of these two demonstrations were the same . . . equal access to jobs.

As soon as CORE's plans were announced, New York City was in a panic. Big celebrities including President Lyndon Johnson were scheduled to speak, as was Robert Kennedy, the former president Kennedy's brother. Two hundred and fifty thousand people were going to attend the Fair's opening on April 22, 1964. If CORE was successful, it would not only disrupt opening day of the Fair, but it would be an embarrassment for the city.

After all the planning, the demonstrations promised to disrupt and ruin what Diana had hoped for . . . a great opening day to the New York City World's Fair and for what? her friends were angry as well. "They will be hurting their own cause," she heard many say. "And for what? Weren't there are plenty of jobs here?" This wasn't the South, after all. It wasn't like the South with its separate drinking fountains, its separate sections for movie-

goers in theaters, its ugly racist faces and vicious dogs. "We are more educat-
ed, more . . . fair, more . . .well more, advanced," Diana and her friends
thought.

For Diana it was *her* Fair and she wanted its opening day to turn out well,
especially because with a few friends Diana decided to take Wednesday,
April 22 off from school and go to the Fair's opening day!

Diana couldn't wait. The whole evening before the Fair's opening she
was as jumpy as a hungry frog in a pond filled with slowly moving flies. she
just couldn't sit still and she certainly couldn't sleep. After all the articles, all
the days watching the Fair take shape, Diana was going to be at the Fair's
opening. she just hoped that it would not be disrupted.

Diana met Sam on that cold, wet, and dreary steel gray morning when she
walked to the subway to meet her friends.

"Sam, I'm going to the Fair today. Don't tell my parents."

"You have a good time, Diana and your secret is safe. Oh, and take a
picture of the Unisphere for me. It's the world's largest global structure . . .
140 feet and it weighs 700,000 pounds! It also has three rings around it that
are representing the tracks of Yuri Gagarin, the first man in space, John
Glenn, the first American to orbit the Earth, and Telstar, the first active
communications satellite."

"I just hope that those demonstrators don't ruin the day for everyone."

Sam smiled and rolled his bicycle with the breakfasts, lunches, and dinners of others filling his baskets.

Diana met her friends, Ellen, Vicki, Carole, Viera, and Marie went down
into the subway station. About thirty-five minutes later, with one transfer,
they were there, at a row of flowers leading everybody into "The World of
Tomorrow," the 1964 World's Fair. Heroically standing before them was its
symbol, the Unisphere, the twelve-story high, spherical stainless steel repre-
sentation of the earth that Sam talked about. It looked like it was floating in
space.

On this drizzling November-like day, they ran around the Fair like chick-
ens with their heads cut off, going from pavilion to pavilion . . . Wisconsin's
"World Largest Cheese," the "It's a Small World" attraction at the Pepsi
pavilion where animated dolls and animals frolicked in a spirit of international unity on a boat ride around the world, "Progressland" where an audience
seated in a revolving auditorium and viewed a presentation about the history
and benefits of electricity in the home, the "Ford Magic Skyway," where
Ford cars moved them all through scenes featuring life-sized audio-enhanced
dinosaurs and cavemen.

There were also the now-famous Belgium Waffles and the Illinois State
pavilion where a robotic Abe Lincoln recited his most famous speeches,
including the Gettysburg Address: "Four score and seven years ago our

fathers brought forth on this continent, a new nation, conceived in Liberty, and dedicated to the proposition that all men are created equal."

The crowds were small that day and Diana wasn't sure if it was because of the weather or because of the threat of demonstrations. Diana and her friends did get to see a few of the protestors. There were some picketers in front of the exhibit of a state whose senator threatened to block the civil rights legislation. There were some protestors at the Unisphere. Some fair-goers watched as the protestors chanted for equality and jobs. Some of her friends complained that they were ruining "their" Fair. Some of the Fair's visitors, including Diana and her friends, booed.

The rain began to fall faster and their clothes were now wet, no longer protecting the boys. As the midday turned toward 3:30, the time when they would have gotten out of school, they headed home so as to not call attention to their trip. As they crossed the bridge and looked down at the Parkway, no cars were stalled and the traffic continued as usual. Into the subway station they went and bought an evening newspaper. In those days there were morning and evening papers. Its headline said, "World's Fair Opens Without Hitch As Protest Fails!"

"Yes!" they shouted, happily ready to read the brochures they took from the exhibits and thinking of the story they were going to tell their parents if they saw those same brochures.

It was now fully dark and still drizzling when Diana walked from the subway station and into the street. As she was entered her apartment building, she saw Sam delivering one more load of groceries. Sam was dressed in a loose-fitting raincoat keeping him mostly dry but, Diana was sure, not very warm.

"How was it?" Sam asked.

"Great," Diana answered.

"Did you see the Unisphere?"

"It's beautiful," Diana answered. "When are you going?"

"Not sure, what with work and all the kids and grandkids. But glad you had fun."

"Sure," Diana said, watching him ride away.

He went upstairs and her parents were waiting for him.

"How was the Fair?"

How did they know everything?

Diana ate dinner and afterward went into her bedroom, laying out all the brochures from each exhibit on her bed. All seemed to have the same theme in slightly different ways . . . how technology was going to build the world we always dreamed of having. There would be, according to the brochures, robots to clean our houses, machines to clear the Amazonian rain forests and use the material they cleared to make new roads and these innovations would

lead to a world where opportunities for leisure time was available for everyone.

But as Diana looked through the brochures, and thought about the Gettysburg Address, the demonstrations for jobs and equality, and the tourists', her
friends', and her own reactions to the protests, she wondered on this cold,
wet late afternoon, if Sam, one of the smartest people she knew, would ever
be able to take advantage of this wonderful world of tomorrow.

QUESTIONS FOR STUDENTS

- Why did the thought at the end of the story cross Diana's mind?
- Why should Diana care about anyone else's situation in life?
- Why did Diana's opinion about the demonstrators at the Fair seem to
  change after she saw Sam on the way home from the Fair?
- What does "fairness" mean and is it important to you and if so, why?
- Do you think that people had a right to demonstrate at the Fair and to
  potentially disrupt something that was very important to a lot of people?
- Did Diana and her friends and the tourists have a right to be angry with the
  protestors?
- How do you think change is made in our world? How would you go about
  it?
- Did you ever feel like you wanted to be involved in helping folks who you
  didn't know? Where do you think that feeling comes from?
- Can we be happy when others suffer?

THOUGHTS FOR STUDENTS

In some ways it is kind of mysterious why Diana became interested in the
Southern civil rights movement of the 1960s. After all, she didn't live in the
South, had no friends from the South, and was not African American. And
yet the powerful images on TV combined with her experiences with African
Americans at camp woke him up to how African Americans were treated.
Understanding how segregation worked in the South didn't make sense. The
more she knew, the angrier she became.

We all seem to have a "built-in" sense of empathy or caring for those
whom we feel are being treated poorly or who find themselves in unfortunate
situations. Think about how seeing the suffering because of floods, terrorism,
war, drought, and famine affects us. Think how even pictures of a suffering
animal stranding on an ice floe makes us feel.

Many people have written about empathy and compassion and it seems to
be a fact of human nature. We are simply "programmed" to feel the joys and
sorrows of others. Diana's connection to the civil rights movement demon-

strated that with modern communication, the ability to see and to feel what was occurring miles away, instantaneously, could and did provoke strong feelings.

However, Diana seemed to have a little problem, didn't he, when suddenly her empathy was challenged when something she cared about could be compromised and he, not others, could be inconvenienced? At first she denied that there could be any racial problems in New York City and felt that the protests might not be necessary. It was not until she saw Sam that evening coming home from the Fair that she understood that the protestors might be making a good point, telling the world that a form of segregation existed in the North too. she understood, for the first time, that the promise of progress, which was, after all, the theme of the Fair, might not be granted to everyone.

Can we be happy when others are suffering? What do you think? Maybe yes, maybe no? When there is poverty, when people are suffering through famine, wars, discrimination, violence, and so on, we all are able to feel their pain, aren't we? But even when we don't directly feel the pain of others, there are ways in which we are all affected by it.

I've been to countries where there are a few rich people and many, many poor people. The rich often live trapped inside gated communities, with armed guards at their doors. When they drive, they are always on the lookout for carjackers. Their heads are continually filled with the fear that those "without" will be trying to take what they don't have from those who do. The wealthy as a result are ultimately restricted and limited, not nearly as deeply as someone in poverty, but restricted nonetheless by the isolation and fear that results from their system of economics, governance, and control. We need to remember that we are truly all in this together and that as long as one part of our world is not comfortable, no part will be.

The empathy we feel toward others is how our psychic and physical connections to each other is experienced. This connection is very, very real. The air someone pollutes is the air we all will breathe. The water we pollute is what we all will drink. Someone's sickness, untreated, could spread to others. Studies have shown that if our friends are happy it will make us happier.

When Diana first felt empathy for those involved with the civil rights movement in the South and later for Sam, it was an entry point into the understanding of how we are all connected and dependent upon each other for our health and happiness.

THOUGHTS FOR TEACHERS

Curriculum and Pedagogical Suggestions: History, Service Learning, Philosophy, and Economics

Engaging students in "real-world" issues and helping them notice how the world is visible in their own backyards is a valuable exercise. Middle school students especially are very interested in moral and philosophical issues and love to think about and discuss contemporary political and social issues, especially those where there are built-in ambiguities.

Wonderfully engaging issues are everywhere. For instance, everyone loves to have nice clothes at affordable prices. Considering how, where, and by whom those clothes are produced can really be a wake-up call for your students. Students will be forced to consider how people producing clothing for Western markets and their landscapes are treated and often exploited and compromised.

What if we looked at the true costs of keeping a four-bedroom, suburban house air-conditioned and heated, even when its inhabitants are not present? How about land development choices? Can we, as a society, still afford to live so far away from schools and services with our three-car garages and big backyards of chemically aided grass? Are we willing to take a little less "comfort" to think and act with the "long term" in mind?

Looking at the long-term effects of our choices is essential for students to develop an understanding that behavior has consequences. Does our temporary "feel-good" behavior produce the long-term results we want, or does it ultimately create the opposite? Was lashing out at someone who you thought purposely pushed you in the hallway beneficial to you in the long run? Was arming vast numbers of Afghan freedom fighters to fight the Russians, who later became the same people who harbored those who planned the World Trade Center bombing, a good idea? Interesting issues . . . short- vs. long-term considerations.

Preparing your students to be positively engaged in our civic world should also prepare them to be active in the creation of their personal lives and for making personal choices as well. It is important to not only engage your students in the great social issues of our times, but also to clearly make the connection between the great global and the great personal issues.

In the late sixties, in the days of second-generation feminism, there was a phrase, as appropriate today as it was almost fifty years ago: "The personal is political." This understanding should inform your choices and your students' choices. Following the long-term consequences of our personal behavior can only set the stage for a more compassionate and ecologically committed citizenry, one that understands the connection between personal decisions and unintended personal and global consequences.

Conclusion

Thank you for reading *A Holistic Approach for Cultural Change: Character Education for Ages 13–15*. I hope that you liked it. Here are a few ideas to help you keep it together and to help everyone, including yourself, feel happier and more comfortable in school and out.

- Think for a second before you let anger or frustration dictate your behavior. Take a deep breath. Walk away. Make a joke. Hum a song. It doesn't matter which technique you use; just find a way to delay acting until your rational side takes control over your emotional response. The truth of your initial reaction melts like an ice sculpture on a sunny summer day when you have a little time to reflect.

  Don't be fooled by the power and false certainty of your initial reaction. Immediate reactions are like a little kid who won't shut up. "Me, me! Pay attention to me! Do what I tell you to do! Do what I tell you to do! Listen to me! I'm right!" Don't worry. Eventually this little kid gets tired of screaming, as long as you don't feed it by acting on its advice. In fact, if you feed it, it becomes hungrier! The most important thing you can do when you are angry, frustrated, or feeling hurt or disrespected is to consider the long-term effects of your action. Ask yourself this question: Will this really get me what I want?

- Decide that you will not bully or tease others to enhance your power or status, nor will you use others as punching bags to make you feel better when you are angry or down. Not only does no one deserve to be treated badly, not only would *you* not want to be used in that way, but also this type of behavior won't get you what you're after.

Bullying or teasing a weaker person does not enhance your reputation. You will appear weaker, less in control, and more insecure. The temporary rush you might get when you trip, push, or tease someone disappears very quickly.

Negative behavior or hating not only won't solve whatever emotional issues you think it might cure, but it also covers up what you are actually feeling and makes it more difficult to see what your real problem is and how you might successfully deal with it. Ask yourself what's really bothering you and why you feel it necessary to export your bad feelings to another person. What are these feelings of sadness, tensions, and insecurities that are stoking your anger? Where are they coming from, and what would be a healthier way for getting your real needs met?

- Remember, you are never invisible to yourself or to others. I know that sounds funny, but what I mean is that when you stand around and allow others to be bullied or teased, or when you join in on the fun, you are affecting the situation, and of course, you will ultimately be affected yourself. Standing by while others are teased or bullied, passing on a rumor, or purposely isolating someone is a strong and very visible statement of support for that action. It isn't easy to do otherwise. I know that from firsthand experience. Remember, courage is not about acting without fear but about recognizing the fear as you act to make another person's life better and you feel more powerful.

- Practice the joy of giving. Giving can be as simple as a short "How are you doing?" to someone who is down or as large as asking someone to participate in a game or to dance at a party when you sense they feel left out. Giving can mean helping out in a soup kitchen or teaching a skill to someone. It can mean standing up for someone who is being picked on or really listening and commenting on another kid's suggestions while you are his or her coworker in a group. It doesn't matter how you give to others; just remember that the more you give, the better and larger you feel.

- Appreciate the importance of your story. You are unique, interesting, complex, and a gift to those around you. We are all important, with lots to share and to contribute. Having the confidence to be who you really are is essential if your little part of the jigsaw puzzle of life is going to play its role in completing and also changing the grand puzzle. We all have our insecurities. Recognize them in yourself, and don't be afraid of them. Don't feel superior when you recognize insecurity in others. Remember, we all have our weak spots, and understanding that, try to create a culture in which we all feel OK about ourselves, even with our vulnerabilities and insecurities.

- Have a good time. Play music. Read. Play sports. Take walks in the city or in the woods. Go to the beach. See art. Get together with friends. Watch a sunset. Go on a roller coaster. See the sunrise. Watch a storm come in. Plant a garden. Fix a car. Build a shelf. The more you take in the wonders of the world, the better you'll feel. The better you feel, the less important real or imagined slights, grudges, hurts, jealousies, envies, and resentments will seem. It is difficult to hold on to old anger when you are looking at a mountain lake at sunset. It is difficult to hold on to a grudge when you are effortlessly skating over a frozen pond.

• Remember, while it is difficult to change your own behavior, it is more difficult to change the behavior of others. Your responsibility is ultimately to yourself, making choices that fill you with energy, joy, surprise, and awe. Doing so will help you make decisions that will have long-term rather than short-term benefits, decisions that will help you create the kind of world you want to be part of. Remember, we're all in it together!

Good luck, and it was fun to spend some time with you.

CONCLUSION FOR TEACHERS

For every problem, there is opportunity—at least that is what wise folks say. Whether bullying is as big a problem as it is portrayed, it doesn't really matter. It does, nonetheless, affect many people. This gives all of you an opportunity to reframe your school-based discussions about character issues from admonition to those that can unite a school community around a shared interest in creating a culture of caring based on mutual benefit.

Our culture's current interest in school character issues comes at a time when wealth disparity in the United States is nearly exceeding all previous levels in history. It is occurring at a time when we seem unable to collectively decide that we must take action to stop or at least slow global warming. It is coming at a time of vast economic change, where a large part of our country's economy is based on Ponzi schemes and derivatives rather than manufacturing for the needs of its citizens. It comes at a time when more and more money is being stored in offshore hiding places that permit the wealthy to avoid contributing to the society into which they were born, where their talents were nurtured, and where they benefited from the work of previous generations. It comes at a time when political extremism threatens to tear the United States apart.

Attention to character education comes at a time when our entire country, not just our schools, is confronting who we are, the choices we are making, and whether our priorities and behavior should be altered. It is coming at a time when the results of acting from a shallow individualism—taking what you want, how you want, without regards to the long-term consequences for you, your family, and your world—is bringing our country and indeed our globe to the brink of destruction, slow or fast, depending on which kind of apocalypse you intellectually and emotionally favor. Consequently, as you approach these character issues in our schools, please understand that you are, with the proper depth and commitment, teaching nothing less than a rethinking of our culture's priorities and behavior, literally before it is too late.

None of us, anywhere on the earth, can any longer pretend that our individual actions have no consequences for the rest of us. Our work on character issues must make everyone a stakeholder in the effort to redirect behavior on both the individual and global levels. By teaching your students about character issues from the perspective of our interdependency within a closed system, we are teaching what it means to be responsible for our planet's future.

Here are some ideas for how you might extend the issues and suggestions discussed in this book:

- Use the stories and talking points in this book as jumping-off points for a school-wide conversation about behavioral issues.
- Allow your students to consider and suggest classroom and school policies for creating a culture where everyone feels supported and safe.
- Create a school-wide "Congress of Stakeholders" that includes all those who have a stake in the culture of the school (teachers, administration, lunch room and janitorial staff, parents) to address problems concerning bullying and teasing and their possible remediation.

    For instance, do students want to allow teasing? What kind of teasing is problematic, and how does one determine that some forms of teasing are friendly, while others are adversarial and violence-provoking? What should school policy be toward the type of teasing your community wants to eliminate? What should be the consequences of behavior that disregards these policies in general? How should consensus be reached? How should these policies be publicized? What are some ways to encourage compliance? How can these ideas and policies be continued and, if needed, altered year to year? How can you communicate with other schools in your area so that you can arrive at a consistent approach within your district and community?

There are many school-based mandates and lots of things that must be accomplished in a very limited amount of time. Making even minor changes to what and how you teach in order to emphasize how much we all have in common is a good start. Find opportunities to emphasize cooperation. Be aware of how you treat your students, staff, and peers; how respectfully you speak; how you defuse potential conflicts; how you share your laughter and attention; and how you solicit your students' thoughts and ideas.

Tell your own stories about how you bullied, were bullied, were teased, were left out, left others out, or passed rumors and how it affected and still has an effect on you.

Good luck with your work, and please know that no one minimizes the difficulty of what you do, underestimates your commitment, or fails to recognize the daunting task ahead for all of us.

A BONUS STORY FOR COMPLETING THIS BOOK . . . FOR STUDENTS AND TEACHERS!

The student asked her master, "What is the difference between heaven and hell?"

The master thought for a second and traveled with the student to a house where its inhabitants were sitting around a table filled with food. Surprisingly, people were starving. Their elbows were locked by a mysterious ailment and would not bend, and while they could grab the food in front of them, they were unable to bring it to their mouths.

Then the master brought the student to another house. It, too, was populated by people sitting at a table filled with food. These people were also afflicted with the mysterious ailment that left their elbows locked and unable to bend. But these people were all well-fed and happy. Like those in the other house, they, too, were able to grab the food in front of them, but unlike the others, they didn't try to feed themselves; instead, with their outstretched arms, they turned to their neighbors and fed each other.

May we all live inside such a banquet.

About the Author

Marc Levitt works at the intersection of the arts, education, and humanities. Mr. Levitt has been an author and storyteller for more than thirty years, and his work as a consultant and performer has taken him to more than sixty countries. His international work has been featured in the *New York Times*. Mr. Levitt has written *Putting Everyday Life on the Page: Inspiring Students to Write, Grades 2–7* (2009), a book about the teaching of writing. He created and directed for five years the innovative Charles N. Fortes Museum Project, based on site-specific education and funded by NEH/Disney Learning Partnership. For sixteen years, Mr. Levitt was the coproducer and host of the national award-winning radio show *Action Speaks! Underappreciated 20th-Century Dates That Changed America*. His two films, *Stories in Stone*, about the Narragansett stone wall–building tradition, and *Woven in Time: The Narragansett Salt Pond Preserve* have been broadcast on PBS stations throughout the United States. Two of Mr. Levitt's audio recordings, *Tales of an October Moon* and *Johnny Appleseed: Gentle Hero*, have both garnered awards and positive reviews.

www.ingramcontent.com/pod-product-compliance
Lightning Source LLC
Chambersburg PA
CBHW020357270326
41926CB00007B/482